ISBN 978-1-332-22140-0
PIBN 10300293

1 MONTH OF
FREE
READING

at

www.ForgottenBooks.com

By purchasing this book you are eligible for one month membership to ForgottenBooks.com, giving you unlimited access to our entire collection of over 700,000 titles via our web site and mobile apps.

To claim your free month visit:

www.forgottenbooks.com/free300293

English
Français
Deutsche
Italiano
Español
Português

www.forgottenbooks.com

Mythology Photography **Fiction**
Fishing Christianity **Art** Cooking
Essays Buddhism Freemasonry
Medicine **Biology** Music **Ancient**
Egypt Evolution Carpentry Physics
Dance Geology **Mathematics** Fitness
Shakespeare **Folklore** Yoga Marketing
Confidence Immortality Biographies
Poetry **Psychology** Witchcraft
Electronics Chemistry History **Law**
Accounting **Philosophy** Anthropology
Alchemy Drama Quantum Mechanics
Atheism Sexual Health **Ancient History**
Entrepreneurship Languages Sport
Paleontology Needlework Islam
Metaphysics Investment Archaeology
Parenting Statistics Criminology
Motivational

THE SUSSEX FOWL.

By S. C. SHARPE.

Part Author of "Progressive Poultry Culture."

Secretary of the Sussex Poultry Club.

Secretary of the Poultry Section of the Sussex County Agricultural Society.

Instructor at the Agricultural and Horticultural College, Uckfield, for 12 years.

Instructor and Inspector in Poultry and Rabbit Keeping under the East Sussex County Council since 1901.

Chairman Table Poultry Test and Member of Council of the National Utility Poultry Society, Westminster.

Originator of the "Light Sussex."

INDEX.

ILLUSTRATIONS.

INDEX TO COLOURED PLATES.

SYNOPSIS OF SIDE NOTES.

FOREWORD.

There are many who can write about Poultry in general, but few who have the knowledge—both from the historic and economic point of view—like S. C. Sharpe, whose name has been so long associated with this grand breed. It is, therefore, with the greatest pleasure that I write a few words, on what is not only a good book, but one that has come to stay. The old, old question of what is the best breed will to many be answered in this work. Eggs, we know, are always wanted, but the foreign competition in the future is bound to severely compete. For the best table birds, combined with fecundity, the home market will for long have a practical monopoly, and there is room for a large extension in this direction.

Just one word of warning : do not let our breeders of Sussex or our judges of exhibition stock get away from type. Type *first, last, and all the time.* The bird, however beautiful in feather, is useless to the breeder if in-kneed or narrow. Furthermore, size or bone is not, in the opinion of the writer, nearly so important as some critics have led us to infer. The book should be read by all true lovers of English fowl, the illustrations carefully studied, and a unanimous vote of thanks passed to the Author for the many years of patient and efficient work that is now made available for all. Increased production is the real road to the recovery of the nation, and it is by that means only that the country will once more take its rightful place in the civilised races of mankind.

T. R. ROBINSON.

July, 1920.

3, Vincent Square, Westminster, S.W. 1.

INTRODUCTION.

"Let me do what good I can while I can, for I shall not pass this way again."

In writing this book my aim is to give those who are interested in poultry "facts" on one of the most handsome and useful varieties of fowls that can to-day be found. My whole life being spent among the research and teaching of poultry culture has given me opportunities of watching the growths of the different varieties and sub-varieties of poultry which have, during the past 30 years, been introduced, and I am able to say, without contradiction, that the "Sussex" have, since their inauguration, moved to the highest plane in the shortest time, and, in my opinion, based on the knowledge of the breed, it has come to "*stay*," and to form our most popular breed of "all-round egg and table fowl." My wish is that in writing this standard work on the "Sussex," it will be helpful to many who, in the future, take up the breed, and to those who are "old hands," it may also be of use at times, and find a corner in the library. I would like to thank all those ladies and gentlemen who have so kindly allowed me to take photos of their birds, and also for the fine specimens which I have had specially sketched and painted by Mr. Wippell, who came down into the County of Sussex and Surrey to carry out the work. All these beautiful coloured plates are from actual winners during 1919, and so I say my thanks are due to :—My old friend, Mr. A. J. Falkenstein, Mr. J. B. Bunney, Mrs. M. A. Grant, Mr. Godfrey W. H. Ellis, Mr. G. E. Howard, Mr. Francis Barchard, J.P., Mr. Hugh McIlveen, and Mrs. Ferguson (Poultry Manager, Mr. P. Shirwin), all of whose birds are represented.

S. C. S.

"Meadham," Lewes.
July, 1920.

ALDERMAN JOHN MILES.
"Our President."

To write a book on the "Sussex" and leave out the "points" of our President would be a sin unforgivable. Alderman John Miles, "Father" of the Sussex Poultry Club—yes, I like this title, for can he be less ?—he was at the first meeting of the Club—no, more—he was at the first meeting held before the Club was formed and for 17 years he's seldom missed attending a meeting. I am going right into all the minute books later and I'll give the number of meetings held since the formation of the Club and show how many our good President has attended. Yes, a truly "wonderful" gentleman is our President. He is one of the few men who one *never* hears a word "against," in my many years connection with Alderman John I have always found him "one of the very best," he's what we term a real English Gentleman—always ready to help a good cause—hours of hard work at meetings and a thorough "Chairman," keeping every Committee man to the point, and should he draw away (as Committee men will do) Alderman John has a fine way of pulling him in again and so keeping the business going; this is helpful to a meeting where much business is on the Agenda.

DETAIL.—I never have met a man who could "top" Alderman John for "detail," the slightest error in a report or in the minutes and he sees it—yes, he'll "ferret" out every little point and in his quiet way just ask if "so and so is quite correct;" oh ! he's "great" at this, and many times its helped to keep the work of the Club in line.

At all the many meetings at which I've met Alderman John Miles, only once do I remember seeing him get a "little irritable;" it was on the 4th September, 1903. The meeting, which lasted from 7 to 10 p.m., and the whole of the time was devoted to "fixing a Standard for the 'Sussex Fowl.'" Yes, although this is 17 years ago, every detail is in my memory; it was a memorable evening scene, and many a time since I have said that instead of "fixing that Standard" in three evenings (we had three meetings over this Standard) we should have taken three years, for it is a feature far too important to pass over quickly. Well, it was during this meeting that Alderman John began to "see red" as hour after hour passed and we got no further than "wing bow," a solid patch of deep glossy brown, or, "Plumage," dark chestnut brown, allowing for greater depth of colour on saddle and wing bow, which should be glossy, and so on. We would get a remark from Alderman John—Well, gentlemen, now which is it to be, wing brown, glossy, did you say? oh! chestnut brown, why no. Walnut brown. Well, come along, gentlemen, we must get on, we can't sit here all night, you know; what are we going to do about this "Wing bow?" Oh! you say now you don't want it brown, you want it dark red; no, I don't care what you have, have it quite red if you like, but let us get on with it. Now, gentlemen, which is it to be? Oh! light brown, no dark brown; now, gentlemen, is that carried? Eh, what, not settled yet! Oh! dear me, gentlemen, time is getting on, and we really can't stay here all night; have we finished yet about the "Wing bow?" I say, Mr. Sharpe, you'd better ask the gentlemen to have some refreshment for time is getting on and we *must* have something before we go, for I'm sure we've all earned it. I have never had such a "doing" in all my life. This wing bow business is irritating, Mr. Sharpe, and I really don't know why you make so much

fuss over it and take up such a lot of time, because time
is valuable, you know, and I really think to-night we
have wasted much, why, the idea of it, colour of the wing
bow, what does it matter whether it is white or black or
chestnut or mahogany, the bird, when roasted and on the
table, will be no better to carve or to eat, it will not
improve the "flavour," and he added, "For to my mind,
Mr. Sharpe, the 'Sussex Fowl' cannot be improved
much as a table bird for good flavour." I remember this
as if only last evening, and one can understand a Chairman getting a little "nervy" going through for hours such
(to one who had never kept any fowls of any kind)
"piffling" work as colour of "Wing bow." No,
Alderman John has never been a fowl keeper, and its
therefore all the more "wonderful" that he should take
such a keen interest in the Club, and all its doings, and
never once has he missed when a special subscription had
been wanted either for support at a Club Show, or County
Agricultural Show, or a Cup fund. Alderman John is
always there first, and a ready first to dip down, and deep
too, into his pockets to give the needful help, and generally
a quiet word something like this—"Well, here's a little
subscription to go on with, and I say, Mr. Sharpe, if you
find that the funds do not come in quite as you
expect, let me know won't you, and I shall be pleased to
give a little more, you know, for I think it's a good cause,
Mr. Sharpe, and I like to help a good cause ; why only the
other day a poor woman came to me, you know, Mr.
Sharpe, she was a poor creature who had worked very
hard all her days, and it was a very deserving case, at least
I thought so, and she," and so on. That's our good old
Alderman John to a "point" And yet another word
of our good President. For several years we have held
our Club Show at the "Palace" and a right good Club
Show it was too altogether in the early days, for we
have not been to the "Palace" since the war broke out.

Never once did Alderman John miss an attendance at the "Palace;" we used to have a general meeting of the Club members during the Show week, and a goodly crowd did we get; it is here where we used to meet our dear old friend, Dr. J. E. Shaw, of Clifton, Bristol, a real help, backer, and good supporter of the Club. I think "a lot" of the Doctor, he's such a kindly sort, and has been one of the greatest "supporters" we have had; he's the kind of doctor you know that makes one feel, if they lived in his practice, they would not mind being ill, because there would be the kindly old Doctor to come along and put me right, and have a chat and a cheery word—would that there were more of his kindly manner and disposition, that alone makes one get well. He breeds some good Reds too, and always supports the shows whenever asked.

Mrs. George Whiteley, of Downton, too, we used to meet, and hosts of other long distance members who were too far away to get to our Annual General Meetings —yes, we had a gathering of the Clans in those days at the "Palace," and when I used to meet Alderman John on Lewes Station, No. 2 Platform, wet, fine, or foggy, not minding the weather, he would say: "Hullo, Mr. Sharpe, I'm pleased the day has come around again for our pleasant trip to the Palace. I have seen the paper this morning, and I noticed our old friend Mr. Bunney is in it again; I'm glad he has won something, and I shall go and see his birds directly I get to the show." And lunch we used to have, a nice little lunch together we two, and a good smoke before going into the meeting. They were pleasant times indeed and not to be forgotten. I could go on writing of "Our President" for hours, but I must only add that Alderman John Miles has the heartiest thanks and good wishes from every member of the Club, and may he live long to see the Club gain in strength and popularity and to show that the many hours spent in committee meetings and in other workings of the Club has put forth the good that he has always hoped for. This and far more, if it could be written, is I know the heartfelt wish of every member of the Club, and I feel that in years and years to come, when we all have ''gone over,'' the good name of Alderman John will remain and be spoken of in kindly remembrance by all who breed the ''Sussex.'' I raise my hat to you, good sir, and wish you long life and good health.

CHAPTER I.

MY FIRST IMPRESSION OF THE SUSSEX FOWL.

It dates back to my childhood days.   I have always been associated with the "Sussex," and although, as I shall show in later chapters, that some of the well-known poultry authorities of the old days wrote letters to me, and wrote to the press, saying there was no such breed and setting up every kind of opposition to the formation of a Club, and saying that they could not be standardized, and all that kind of thing.   Yet, I had bred them as a lad, and had sent them to County Wexford, Ireland, and Kilkenny and Antrim, and, in fact, to many parts of Ireland years and years before ever a thought was given to forming a club.   I had bred the three colours in those days, but, of course, they were not true either to colour or type, because no thought was given to this, the point being eggs and table, and it was winter eggs, too, and it was in this work that I found and proved the value of the Light Sussex—but of that later.   In the old days one could see on many farms in Kent, Surrey and Sussex a class of bird such as no other county in England kept. One could drive through a part of the county and see thousands and thousands of strong, heavy framed, "square shouldered"—yes, that's the word, square-shouldered—young cockerels and pullets in the early spring, and in some districts particularly these would mostly consist of "white" or what to-day is called the Light Sussex.   Note that I said "Early Spring Chickens."   Now, here is a point to remember.   The

The Light Sussex.

Early Spring Chicken.

Light Sussex was always a good winter layer, and this is shown by the number of early chickens which we used to raise—had they not been a good, yes, an exceptionally good winter layer, how would the chicken rearers have been able to get out their hundreds of early spring chickens ?

There are many people to-day, I think, who believe that most of the chickens which used to be reared for the London Markets were bred in the Heathfield district of Sussex, but such was not the case. Heathfield was the great fattening centre. We might term it the great "finishing" centre, where the chickens were brought to be crammed and finished off for the market, but the chickens were mostly reared in Kent in those days, many very large rearing farms being run and many thousands of chickens reared which eventually found themselves at the "Derby," for this was the **Chicken for the Derby.** great aim to get as many as possible "out" early and feed them well and get them ready for the fatteners so they could be on the market for that great event. This, too, meant the highest prices paid during the season and for the youngest and smallest bird, so that it was "money" both ways for the breeder, for a small bird would mean less cost of feeding and extra price.

In going through these large "chicken" farms one would see all sorts of colours, but, as I have before re- **A Mixture of Colours.** marked, some would specialize more in the light variety, but I well remember breeding a bird—I only wish I had the breed now—a chick that was very fast growing and very strong and sturdy, the colour being something like a barred rock, but the ground colour was much lighter, a most excellent table bird, and I've never seen anything like it or that could compare with it. Had we only known in those days that the "Sussex" would be a standard breed ! I well know there would have been another variety which to-day would have given even the Lights a "shake up."

Feather Legs.   There was much said about the feather on the legs of the Sussex in the old days, and some even went so far as to write me, saying the feather on the legs would never be bred out, but I well know that when breeding what was then called the White Sussex fowls, the larger percentage of them were quite free from feather, and to-day one gets very few with any sign of feather.

CHAPTER II.

THE FORMATION OF THE SUSSEX CLUB.

The Sussex Club was formed in the old County Town of Lewes, where I am now writing, and it came about in a strange manner. A meeting was held in the town at which Mr. Edward Brown was speaking, and in the course of his remarks he mentioned to the farmers that they had Southdown Sheep and Sussex Cattle, but no breed of poultry of a special Sussex character, but this remark was not tolerated by some of those present, and Mr. E. J. Wadman, who is a large and well-known farmer, spoke up and put quite a different light on the matter, saying that for years he had bred a bird uniform in colour and type, a Red Plumaged bird, and that he should call it a Red Sussex, and further that he would have a "talk" to a few other poultry keepers in the neighbourhood and they would show Mr. Brown that there was such a bird as the "Sussex." From this there was frequent discussion on the subject at markets and meetings, and the whole matter became aired, with the result that it got into the press, then things began to look lively, letters appeared in the local papers and in The Poultry Press, from some who were "dead" against bringing the "Sussex" into the Exhibition Net. "Oh," said they, "the good old Sussex will be ruined, it is a 'table' bird, and what is the value of colour of feather on a table fowl? Why spoil a breed which has been reared in this and one or two other counties just for the sake of winning a 'Card' at a show!" The letters of this kind, many of which I have on my desk as I write, would fill a

Opposition to forming a Club.

good sized cabinet. Here is the copy of a letter from Mr. Harrison Weir, a gentleman of great reputation and well known. This letter was written just after the formation of the Club and Standards, and one may note what he says about the "many" colours, and in the opinion of this gentleman, five toes in the Sussex should be allowed, in fact I've letters before me from people saying we should never breed out the five toes, Kent and Sussex Fowls always had five toes, and the Kent and Sussex fowls always *would have* five toes, but we found it quite easy, and in three years where the breeders had been careful in mating, the fifth toe had disappeared and to-day one never sees a chick with this peculiarity.

POPLAR HALL, APPLEDORE,
KENT.
OCTOBER 2ND, 1903.

"I am much honoured by your asking me to be a Vice-President of the Sussex Fowl Club, but I am sorry to say that I cannot join it as I am opposed to it and intend writing against it. I do not agree with your limit of colour, nor did the best class of fowl have but four toes. Both my late brother and myself knew the bird well— very well—for over 74 years, and certainly they were of many colours. Nor is it politic to limit the colour or colours of *any table fowls*. Also, why was Kent left out and Surrey put in ? I am very sorry, very, but you must excuse my joining what I am decidedly adverse to.

"I am, dear Sir,
"Yours truly,
"HARRISON WEIR."

What would Mr. Tegetmeier say now if he were breeding Sussex and getting orders for birds at £10 to £50 each ? Certainly his words have come true as to making money out of the breed, and doesn't this apply to all kinds of stock that one breeds for exhibition ; surely a man deserves some kind of recompense if he spends much of his time and brain in the proper and careful selection of stock, to breed in the best points and to breed out the bad, he is doing a good and useful work for the country in which he lives, and so in my opinion he is entitled to what benefit he may be offered. Had the Club taken the advice given them—"this wet blanket" advice in 1903, there would have been no " beautiful high bred Sussex" to-day, but only those Kent and Sussex Chickens of many colours and many hues ; yet even so, we have standardized this breed and still have a champion table fowl. I also have another letter by me, written in the Summer of 1903, and the amazing part about this is, this gentleman, a large landowner and farmer in the heart of East Sussex, says in his letter, that there is no need for a Club, that such an idea is preposterous, and will do no end of harm to a most useful class of table chicken. He goes on to say that there is no such thing as a Sussex Fowl, and never has been. That the "Higglers" do not want feathers, they want meat, and if a Club is formed it will be worse than damnation. We had bred fowls for many years, but as to there being such a thing as the Light Sussex it's all too absurd, and this good man finishes up with "I shall do all in my power to stop *you* from getting a lot of 'Fanatics' (not Fanciers) to join together and call themselves a "Sussex Club."

I have more of this sort of matter on my desk, but will leave it at this, and so you see, this was the kind of encouragement one got from some of the breeders in the County, and I may just add I could quote more than one such letter from people who to-day are breeding hundreds of high class Sussex, and making good money from them. Needless to say these dear people "play another

A Sussex Yeoman.

B

tune'' to-day and more than one claim in the press
to have been somewhat instrumental in bringing the
breed forward, such is the perversity of some Englishmen.

CHAPTER III.

THE FORMATION OF THE CLUB.

After many meetings and much discussion and letters in the Press, a meeting was called on the 23rd July, 1903, at the Elephant and Castle Hotel, Lewes (the County Town of Sussex) for the purpose of forming a Sussex Poultry Club. Those present were Alderman John Miles, voted to the Chair, Messrs. W. W. Morris, G. Cripps, G. Cox, A. J. Cox, S. Langridge, P. G. Hughes, A. Cottrill, sen., and A. J. Cottrill, junr., S. Pitcher, A. J. Langridge, D. Roberts, and S. C. Sharpe.

The meeting was held in conjunction with the Lewes Fanciers' Association, and after some discussion Mr. W. W. Morris proposed, and Mr. Cottrill, senr., seconded "That a Sussex Poultry Club be formed to fix a standard for Sussex Fowls with a view to improving the breed," the above twelve gentlemen becoming "Members," and offering to support and give all possible assistance, and here let me say, strangely, only *two* of these were breeders, however, that may be so, yet it was this start of the stream—which to-day, at the time of writing, has become a river—and will, I hope, yet grow into a very wide and fast moving river. The Secretaries appointed at this meeting were Messrs. A. J. Cox and A. J. Langridge, although the latter, a very dear friend of mine and loved by all who knew him, lost his life in France in 1916.

Messrs. A. J. Cox and A. J. Langridge.

Mr. A. J. Cox is now a Life Member of the Club and still taking a lively interest in its working and great thanks and praise are due to him for

Work of the
Secretary, Mr.
A. J. Cox.

the very heavy duties he performed during those first days of the young Club work, which he did with the greatest care and diplomacy, and it needed much of this in those early days. Mr. Langridge was unable to put in so much time, although he too helped and took a live share, but the brunt of the work fell on to Mr. Cox, and looking at the first Minute Book and Accounts, as I am doing now, I feel that much is due to Mr. A. J. Cox, for the books are most excellently kept. The Minutes, all so clearly and plainly set forth, and the hundreds and hundreds of letters all docketed and filed, all this goes to show how thoroughly he put his heart into the job. He ran the Secretaryship in conjunction with the late Mr. A. J. Langridge, for 2 years, that is 1905, when he gave it up and I was elected the Hon. Secretary, which office I have filled up to the present year 1920. It was on the 21st December, 1905, that the Second Annual General Meeting was held at Headquarters, Lewes, when, on the proposition of Mr. J. Adams, who is now in the great beyond, seconded by

S.C.S. elected
as Secretary.

Mr. J. Bridge, I was unanimously elected Hon. Secretary, and whilst on the subject I may say that I have never regretted taking up the work, for it has been very interesting to watch and to be able to keep in touch with the growth of the Club. I have met many interesting people during my several years of office, and made many good friends. What little criticisms I've ever had I've enjoyed, for it has always been honest, and the Committees together with which I have worked have always been most kind and thoughtful, as well as helpful,

The working
of the
Committee.

and going back through the many meetings we have held (I will give the number later) I do not remember one single case of discord. This says much for the easy and pleasant working of my Committees. On the 30th July, 1903, the

The first
Committee.

first Committee of the Club was formed. I will give the names of the members, and then, on referring to the

"Report and list of Committee and Members for 1920," one will be able to see how changed the names are, in fact, the only two original to-day, with the exception of Mr. W. S. Tucker, are Alderman John Miles and myself. The following were elected on 30th July, 1903.—Messrs. G. J. Lenny, E. G. Hughes, D. Roberts, W. W. Morris, G. Cox, T. G. Cottrill, senr., F. M. Huggett, W. S. Tucker, S. Langridge, A. Uridge, J. Adams, T. Pitcher, T. Cottrill, junr., and S. C. Sharpe. Most of these gentlemen were taken from the Lewes Fanciers' Association, of which I believe all were members of that Committee.

The second Committee meeting was held on the 5th August, 1903, with the view of drawing up the Standard for the breed, but it was decided to wait a few weeks, to get the opinions from various breeders, etc., as to the points, and it was resolved that some breeders be asked to bring birds in to the next meeting, and have a discussion with reference to their various colours and points, Mr. D. Roberts and myself being asked to draft Rules for the Club, these Rules I shall not publish as they can be obtained from the Club and are always published in the Annual Report, which every year can be obtained for a small sum from the secretary of the Club. Between the dates of 5th August and 4th September, several meetings took place, all of which I was able to attend, and I well remember the "trying" times we had in getting out, first a rough standard and pulling it to "bits," then spending more hours trying to make up something "nearer the line," and I may say right here I have many times before remarked, we should have taken three years to form and get out that Standard, instead of three months. Had we done this, we should to-day not have had, as I believe, well, no, I will not say. Anyway, I have many times felt amused when I have heard the "later day man" who has only the last few years taken up the breeding of Sussex, make strong comments on the Club's standard.

Second Meeting

Fixing the Standards.

He little knows the many hours and the difficulties which some of us had before us to get the Standard fixed even roughly, for this is a point I must mention here, for it seems to me very few people seem to recognise, and that is that we are a Club of Four Colours; even in those days of starting we were a Club of "Three," and there is no other Club in England that I know of which is fostering more than one colour, and this fact must not be lost sight of, and this again made the fixing of a standard more heavy because there were three to draw up and fix—not one. Well, on the 4th September a meeting was held at headquarters, Lewes, with the object of fixing the Standards, as it had already been resolved to include the three colours, although I had a very big fight to get the Lights admitted. More as to this anon, the wording was to be, Red or Brown, note the *or*, not *and*, Light and Speckled, this was settled at a meeting held 1st September, 1903. You see we were going very fast, having meetings every few days, and we had *long* meetings too. I do not propose to give the "old standards" but on going through them one finds rather interesting reading, and very different from those which we have just revised and published, but then, we must remember several years have passed and the Club has been "growing" with the times, also that it (the Standard) has been altered three times. Yes, it was not many weeks after "fixing" the first standard that someone wanted an alteration, and I remember that one member, who is now "gone over," was most anxious to get a standard of his own; he was a breeder of Speckled and thought that was the only Sussex, also he tried very hard to have the standard fixed to suit his own type and colour of bird, which no doubt from his point of view would have been all right, but had this gone through and been adhered to, our Speckled Sussex to-day would have been quite a different specimen.

On the 8th September, 1903, another meeting was held, and for several hours we again threshed and ham-mered away at the Standard. Specimens of "Sussex" were brought in to show markings and type, cutting out this and adding that; oh, it was a tiresome job. I ought to add that on several occasions Breeders sent or brought in Light Reds, Speckleds and others, and these were placed on the table and carefully examined for points, and I may say some of them were queer specimens too. I only wish I had taken photos of some of those birds, they would have caused interest if published in this work, and as far as I can remember there were no two birds alike, they not only varied in colour but in type and size, and oh yes, it really was a "motley" crowd that assembled at Headquarters to be examined on points, and I am thinking now that they really did not help much towards getting the Standard fixed for they were too "contra-dictory" and caused much conflict of opinion, because every man who brought a bird or two swore that his was the type, and his was the colour. I often, when thinking of those hours of meetings, marvel that we did not come to blows over the question of colour and type. I well know there were some very heated arguments and the room used to get a flavour of "sulphur." All this, of course, is history, but I like to mention it so that those who are breeding the Sussex to-day and grumble about one or two minor points in the Standards, may remember the very difficult and not too pleasant task that some of us went through in the "pioneer days."

It was at this meeting that it was decided to become affiliated to "The Poultry Club," a step which was rightly taken, and we have all through these years held all our Club Shows under the Poultry Club Rules. Also at this meeting on the 8th September, the Rules were brought forward and adopted, and these Rules have not been "cut about" as have the Standards, but are the same to-day as when we set them out.

Specimens of Sussex brought in to show markings and type.

Affiliation to Poultry Club.

CHAPTER IV.

THE FIRST CLUB SHOW.

First Show of
Sussex.

It has been stated that the Sussex made their debut at the Royal Agricultural Show in 1904, but this is not correct, for they were first penned at the Lewes Fanciers' Association then held in November, 1903. The entries of cockerels were not heavy, and the type and colour, I well remember, were varied, to say the least of it. The Club gave three Silver Medals and the winners were Mr. E. J. Wadman first in Reds, Messrs. E. and H. Russell first in Lights and Mr. G. J. Lenny first in Speckleds ; these were the first medals ever presented by the Club. In these early days there was much discussion as to whether the Speckled

Spangled
Sussex.

should be called the Spangled Sussex, and in one letter I have before me a well-known breeder of that day writes saying he is very pleased to see they are to be called the Spangled Sussex, as he thinks that name far more aristocratic, and that it applies more generally to the bird, but as we know—this name they did not get.

Spangled or
Jubilee
Orpington.

Then, again, there was much written in the press and many letters to the Club with reference to the so-called Jubilee Orpington or Spangled Orpington, and at a meeting held on the 18th November, 1903, a resolution was passed as follows :—"That the Secretaries be directed to have a letter inserted in all the Poultry Papers, pointing out the similarity of the Speckled Sussex and the so-called Jubilee or Spangled Orpingtons, stating at the time that this Club was already affiliated to the Poultry Club. They were also instructed to communicate with the Poultry Club, drawing their attention to the matter, and to say that this Club strongly protested against the Jubilee or Spangled Orpington being recognised as a distinct breed.''

This letter, of course, raised much discussion in the poultry press, and elsewhere, at this time, we had several letters from Mr. Lewis Wright, who took *Mr. Lewis Wright and the* a keen interest in the formation of the Club, and was *Sussex.* asked to act as one of our first judges, but I have a letter before me in which he declines to accept that honour, and goes on to state that although he has written of the ''Sussex,'' and thinks there is a future before them, yet he has never bred a Sussex, and (note this) that *every judge should be a breeder*. I agree with Mr Lewis Wright, for it is only by breeding the bird one can study and get all its points, etc. In a further letter from Mr. Lewis Wright, I notice he gives quite a long history of the White Orpington, which in that *The Albion or White* day was called ''The Albion.'' and was introduced *Orpington.* by Mr. Godfrey Shaw. This, I know, is correct, as Mr. Godfrey Shaw told me himself that he made up the ''Albion'' from the Light Sussex, although at that time it was called White Sussex, and Barndoor and all sorts of ugly names. He made it up by breeding out the black wing and tail feathers, also hackle, which in those days in many birds were very thin, and in some not showing at all.

First Club Show.
The first Club Show was held at the Royal Agri-cultural Show, Wembly Park, in 1904, and it was mainly due to the efforts of Mr. Edward Brown that classes were put on at this great event. After much correspondence between the Secretary of the Royal and this Club, it was arranged that four classes for each variety should be put up, and specials to be granted by the Club. Three of these classes were cancelled

Entries at First Club Show.

owing to insufficient entries, and this left a total entry in nine classes of 47, a somewhat smaller entry than the Club Show in 1919!

Quality of the Exhibits.

Needless to say, there was much criticism of the breed at this Show, and afterwards in the press, many poultry keepers and fanciers saying that the Sussex would never be of any use in the show pen, the specimens shown were all mongrels, and that there was no such thing in the poultry world as an Exhibition ''Sussex;'' all this kind of criticism and irritating letters were being *continually received*, but it made no difference to the enthusiasm of our Sussex breeders beyond the fact that some of us ''pegged'' away the harder to get the breed well known and bred to better type and colour. I made several entries at the first Club Show and took five prizes, including three firsts, and reserve for the medal. Photos of these birds you will see between pages 48 and 49, and they will give a good idea of the ungainly and miserable specimens exhibited at the first Club Show; it will also go to prove what has been done for the breed during the past 17 years.

Shedding Feathers.

A very amusing thing happened at this show. It was held in July, the weather of course was pretty warm, and it being the 1st Club Show, of course some of the exhibitors were ''new hands,'' and so when it came to the question of washing the birds before sending to the Show, some of them were not quite up to the mark, as the following story will show. One exhibitor, whose name I will leave out, had gone to much trouble to wash his birds and get them up for the occasion, but being, as I presume, over anxious to make a thorough job of washing, and doing it well, he made the mistake of using the water too hot, the result being that on the second day of the Show his birds had not a dozen feathers left on them, the pen was covered with feathers outside and in, and the most amusing part of the whole affair was that one of the birds had a first prize card and special put up against it, and the public all clamoured to know on what points the judge made his awards. Oh, it was great fun, and of course was much commented upon in the press.

The winners of the Medals at the First Club Show were as follows :—For the best bird of the Red or Brown Sussex (in these days we used the term Red or Brown and in my opinion it should have been left so, then our Red Sussex would to-day have had black in breast admissible), Mr. David Roberts, Lewes; Best Light Sussex, Messrs. E. and H. Russell, Chiddingly, Sussex; Best Speckled, Mr. Charlie Page, Wilmington, Sussex.

Winners at First of Special Club Show.

CHAPTER V.

THE GROWTH AND PROGRESS OF THE BREED SINCE 1903.

A glance at the photograph showing the Light Sussex Cockerel and Light Sussex Pullet, exhibited at the first Club Show, and then turn to the first Light Sussex at our last Club Show, held at Lewes, in November, 1919, will give the reader a fair idea of what has happened during those years. Note the difference in colour, in type, in breadth and depth; in fact they appeared two distinct types and breeds as shown here, and all this done by careful selection, careful breeding and the blending of the best types and colours together. I shall have more to say on the subject in a further
Mating a fine art.
chapter, but I may state here that the mating of birds to bring out the points required is a fine art, and it is the privilege of few to be able to do this. One must have "an eye" to be able to mate and to know what he is "going for." There must be, or should be, a definite object when making up a pen of, say half-a-dozen hens and a cockerel, and the birds must all have "minute" inspection, the weak point on one side to be strengthened in the other—yes there's much in that. There are many breeders who put down six or eight hens and a male bird at random, saying, "Oh, we ought to get a few good 'uns' from that pen." Too much is left to chance, or luck, as it is called. I say it is not luck which gets the perfect specimen, but care, forethought, judgment, hours spent working out the various "points" of the male and female, this is the only way to get the best

results, and to be sure of getting something right, something which one is aiming for, and so I say the breeding of these fine Sussex, which we have seen in the large Shows during the past year or so, have mostly emanated from just two or three "brains," for where I find one breeder can "mate" his flock I find forty that have no fixed plan or idea at all.

During the war, of course, the Club was not able to do much; the shows were not held and breeding on many farms was suspended, but I am glad to say that everyone who was able to stay in this country and had pens of Sussex, did their best to keep the breed going, and great thanks are due to a few breeders who kept the stock up and even had their Annual Sales. By this means it was possible to get good stock immediately after the war, and hence the fine number of entries made at the large shows when they again got on the move. Had it not been for the courage and foresight of some of these breeders in 1915-16 and 17 our stock would have been very low and two or three years would have been required to get into stride again . I would like, before leaving the subject of "progress, " to make reference to our Annual Market Sale of Sussex. This sale was first started in 1914, with the object of allowing Breeders to clear their surplus stock, and it was held in the Lewes Market. The sale soon created interest, and a better class of bird was sent to the Annual Sale, with the result that last year, 1919, a new feature was brought in, and that was a Show and Sale. One reason for introducing Classes for some of the birds being to induce Breeders to send a better class of Sussex to the sale. Classes were arranged, small entry fees were charged and Silver Specials were awarded, a club judge being engaged to adjudicate. The venture proved a huge success, it drew more people, it drew more birds, and it also drew a far better class of bird. It gave many

Slack during the War, but did not die.

The Annual Market Sale.

Show Sale 1919.

Breeders an opportunity of getting "new blood" for their breeding pens. A stipulation in the schedule, which was good, stated that *all* birds which took prizes must be sold by Auction after the Judging, or the owner would forfeit the prize and silver special if he won one. This, of course, checked the Breeders from buying in their own birds, and so gave other people a chance. The entries were good, over 500 birds being put in the show and sale, and very few, if any, of these were bought in. It is to be hoped that the Annual Show and Sale will continue to grow and become more and more popular every year, as it is helpful to the smaller breeders, by finding a ready outlet and sale for his best surplus stock. The show and sale is already fixed for this year, 1920, to be held in the first week in October.

Early
Hatched
Cockerels.

I would like to add here, perhaps for the benefit of many breeders who do not seem to realise the fact that a male bird if to be used in his first season, should be hatched early (I mean by early, January or February), and that it is doing harm to the Club and to the breed to send half-grown unmatured Cockerels to the Annual Sale. Last year there were certainly a less number of these late hatched cockerels, but it is wrong to send any, far better to put them on the table than keep or sell them for breeding. One does not see this so much in the Pullets, and although a few are sent immatured the majority are pretty fully grown.

CHAPTER VI.

THE SUSSEX AS I KNEW THEM 30 YEARS AGO.

As I shall state in a later chapter, there were a few poultry keepers in 1903, when we were trying to form a Club for the "Sussex," who tried very hard to have one variety only, and that variety to be the "Spangled" or Speckled. For the reds we have much to thank Mr. E. J. Wadman. Of this gentleman more anon, but few people to-day know the work I put in during those days to get the Lights recognised. I could publish many letters which are in front of me now, from people who tried hard to convince everyone there was no such bird as a "White Sussex" as they then called them, the only breed was the Speckled (in their own mind), although they thought they might tolerate a "Red."

Now, I had been breeding those very same "Lights" for years, and my people before me, and knew the value of the birds. I knew the quick growth of the chick and the laying value of the hens, for as winter layers they were excellent, hence the number of early spring chickens one could hatch out from Light Sussex, for I am now writing of the days before the 200 or 270 egg strain, all this has happened years since. I used to keep and breed a fine Speckled bird too, and I also used to see them in the three Counties, Kent, Surrey and Sussex, but never remember seeing or hearing of any being bred in the North or in the West of England. The name given then was White Sussex Fowl, or as in the case of the Speckled, the Speckled Dorking Fowl. In some parts of the Weald of Kent, a "chicken farmer" would breed nearly all Speckled Dorkings, while on other farms they would breed the White Sussex or Reds.

The Sussex in the Eighties.

I do not remember seeing many—and at one time a good deal of crossing with the Buff Orpington was carried out, the result being a much lighter red chick was bred—but in those days colour of feather did not count, it was size of frame, quickness of growth and a white fleshed bird which could be grown along and put into the fattening pen at the age of 12 to 14 weeks, and I have often seen chicks at 11 weeks old in the early spring, caught up and crammed. Being a finished article when only 13 weeks and a day or so from the shell, these were the class of chicken that the chicken farmer was "out" for, and it may readily be understood that where such fast growing breeds could be found, those were the birds which gave the farmer the best profits and quickest returns.

Thousands of Chicken on a Farm.

See Photo in Kent and Sussex Fowl, 1847.

Some of these farms would breed many thousands of these chickens during a season, and it says much for the laying quality of the old Kent or Sussex fowl when I tell you that the chickens were hatched in December, January and February, and all with hens, as there were no machines in the early days, and so it proves this class of bird to be a good winter layer or they would not have had them as broodies.

TYPE OF SUSSEX COCK.

SUSSEX CLUB MARKET SALE, 1915.

LIGHT SUSSEX COCKEREL.
A Club Winner, 1919.

A LIGHT SUSSEX PULLET.
A Club Winner 1919.

LIGHT SUSSEX, reared by Hens

A Light Sussex and Wyandotte Farm.

Light Sussex Cockerel.
Winner, 1919.

LIGHT SUSSEX COCK.

CHAPTER VII.

The Light Sussex.

To-day the most popular variety of Sussex—and, perhaps, I may add the most useful. I often make the remark that the Light Sussex is the nearest bird we have in this Country to an ideal or all-round fowl for egg and table properties combined. In this variety we get these two points, in addition to a handsome-looking bird, for to see a flock of Light Sussex in a meadow when the sun is shining is a sight to remember. Again, they have another very useful quality, and that As Broodies and Mothers. is as broodies and mothers. A Light Sussex when she becomes broody is generally safe to entrust with a batch of eggs, and this in the early season, too, when such cannot be said of many other breeds. She will sit well and when her chicks are out she makes one of the best of mothers, and if the situation admits of it she may be let out of the coop with her young brood, when she will hunt and forage around, finding most of the necessary food for her family. Yes, the Light is one of my favourites as a broody and a mother.

As a winter egg layer, I seldom find her equal. As a layer in Winter. Of course, it is only right to mention here that there is much in "strain" as with all breeds, and some breeds of Light will give better results than others. I have a record here on my desk which I took only last evening when visiting a farm where Lights have been bred for the past 10 years, and a remarkable point about this record is that the birds are all hens (1918 hatched).

C

A little pen of seven, moulted out in August and September, commenced to lay in October. This month, as they were not mated, the poultry man did not keep account of the number of eggs laid for October, but from the 1st November onwards, a record has been kept and it read as follows :—November, 165 ; December, 156; January, 150; February, 143—Total from November to February, 614 eggs from 7 Light Sussex two year old hens. This will show the value of a good laying strain Light for winter work, and these are exhibition birds too. The second prize winning Light at the 1919 Club Show is one of this seven, and she was a pretty good colour and type to take a second in an open class with 52 entries. This is particularly interesting, because we so often find an exhibition fowl is a poor layer, in fact difficult to get eggs from at all. This is only one case of a high egg strain, I could mention many more, but this will suffice, and is right "down to date."

Size of Eggs. We sometimes get complaints from people who start keeping the Lights, with reference to the size of the egg. I have found that some strains, as is the case with all breeds, will lay a rather small egg, but this is more generally to be found when the bird has been laying for several months without a rest. I notice that a pen of Lights which become broody more frequently, lay larger eggs than those which go on laying for several weeks without a little natural rest, and to sum up the question of size of Light Sussex eggs, I say that it is greatly due to the excessive and high fecundity of the variety. I would like to add here that an improvement

How to Improve the Size of the Eggs. is not difficult to make, and for the benefit of those who find the flock laying a low average size or weight, I would say, just make a selection before mating of a Cock or Cockerel for the breeding pen from a pen which

is known to always throw a good size egg. The pullet
from the strain will give a better egg.

The colour of the egg from some of the Lights is Colour of Egg.
rather disappointing sometimes. They vary very much,
some being almost a deep brown, and others nearly
white. I have recently seen seven plates of Light
Sussex Eggs placed out on a table, being a demonstration in colour for the benefit of Students, and not
one of these seven being alike in colour, in fact, most
people would say all seven were from different breeds.
Some were a nice brown, some a very good tint and
others almost white. Of course all this can be altered
if one wishes to do so, for by careful selection of the hens,
and also the selection of a male bird from a pen which is
known to lay a good tint or a brown as the case may
be, one will obtain a mob which will lay the right colour.

I have reared Lights under all sorts of weather The Stamina of the Lights.
and soil conditions. I have sent them to all parts
of the world, from cold Russia to South America,
and to India and Egypt, and I have letters before me at
the moment of writing saying how well the birds have
settled down, and appear to acclimatise themselves
immediately on arrival, so as an export breed they can Export.
be highly recommended. They will stand a change of
weather or a change of soil better than any breed I
know, and this is a very useful point, and makes them
suitable for any climate or situation. Although I have A Rich Egg
mentioned that the Lights lay an egg of many colours,
I should add that the quality is excellent. We know
in these days, of course, that the feeding of the bird
denotes the flavour of the egg, but in some breeds even
then we do not get quite that richness of flavour and
colour of yolk as in others, but in the Lights, giving
good sound feeding and a clean house and run or free
range, the Light Sussex egg is one which will always
be admired on the breakfast table, a truly rich and

meaty egg. So that is another point in favour of this handsome variety.

Fertility.

We generally find the Lights fertilise well, and no doubt this is due to the activity of the breed. They are never a lazy bird, always out early in the morning, when allowed freedom, and always on the hunt for food. This means they do not get over fat, however well fed they may be, and naturally fertility follows. A point in favour of the Lights for early winter rearing, and in tests I have carried out with many breeds during my 12 years work and experiments at the Agricultural College, is the fact that I could always rely upon greater winter fertility amongst the pens of Lights, which again shows us why the old Kent and Sussex fowl was so useful for rearing early winter and spring chickens in years past.

Hardy Chicken.

I have mentioned the usefulness of the Lights as brooding hens, and I may say that I know of no other breed of fowl which is such a valuable sitter. Fifteen eggs may be placed under a Light Sussex broody at any time of the year, providing the nest is properly made, and she will cover them, and if fertile, hatch them all out. The chicks are generally very hardy and strong. Of course, as in any other breed, if the pens, when mated, are not in condition, or are immature, then it would have a bad effect upon the embryo chick, and such chicks would be difficult to rear. But given stamina in the hens and male bird and maturity, I seldom have found chickens of any breed so easy to bring up as the Light Sussex, and this applies to hen or incubator

Colour of the Chicks' Legs.

hatched chicks. The colour of the leg of the newly hatched light is sometimes puzzling to the novice, and I think it only right to make mention here of cases which have come before my notice. On more than one occasion have I been called in to give an opinion on the "purity" of the breed. Eggs having been bought for hatching from some known breeder of Lights and when the chicks hatch out the legs have a distinctly yellow appearance, and as it is one of the great qualities of a "Sussex" to have pure white legs, this, of course, makes the "would be" Light Sussex breeders think there must be a very great error, and that the wrong kind of eggs have been hatched. Such is not the case, however, for it often happens that a batch will throw quite a yellow leg when first out, which goes off in due course, and as the chick grows its white leg shows up. So one need have no qualms on the point when hatching out the first mob of Light Sussex. The body colour, too, sometimes causes alarm. I get letters saying the chicks, instead of hatching out white in colour show a good deal of smuttiness or dark colour. Well, this may be so, but often this disappears with the first moulting of the down. I may say here that one should not get "fretful" if the youngsters do not come out in colour at first like a Palace winner. It should be remembered that they are somewhat like a chrysalis, and have several stages to go through, and as I shall point out in the other varieties of Sussex, they have even a greater variation of colour when first they come to see daylight. I want everyone who intends taking the Sussex up seriously, and with the view of breeding something good for colour and perhaps exhibition, to take special note of these remarks, for it may then perhaps save such a person the trouble of writing an unpleasant letter to the breeder who supplied the sittings of eggs.

Whether reared under hens or in brooders, the chick will be found hardy and fast growing. I prefer the hen for rearing, but, of course, we cannot get sufficient broodies, and at the time of season when we most want them. I have noticed, too, that although we may use an egg for hatching that is not quite up to the size we like, yet when the hatch is due, all the chicks are about equal in size, and unless something happens to give the chick a chill and pneumonia they will generally be quite an even brood right away from the first. We are not so liable to get the minor and common chick ailments in the Sussex as in some breeds, owing to their hardiness, and so for winter and early spring rearing they can be recommended beyond

The Changing in colours. many other breeds. As the chicks get on in growth and age, it will be noticed the body colour often changes considerably. For instance, I have seen chicks which at first have quite a tendency to dark colour after the age of eight weeks come out quite a sound white, and

Do not weed out too early. it is not safe to weed out until they get the new feathering at about 14 to 16 weeks old, and with some of the other colours it is wise to wait even longer. I should like to mention here that where one is "out" for exhibition, it certainly does help matters when the chicks are

Keep free from "Weather." kept from sun, rain and wind. I do not mean to say that they should be shut up entirely, but I do very well know that with the Light especially, and more in the cockerels than the pullets, the sun and rain, or, in other words, the "weather" has a very great effect upon the feathers and top colour. I suggest for all the most promising birds some form of complete shelter, which is moveable and collapsible, so that it can be easily moved to fresh ground, for I much prefer to keep the birds on the ground; if placed in pens in a shed they will develop far too much comb, and this is a part of the bird we do not want to force. Short strong grass is the best place to put the growing cockerels and pullets, and if moved pretty often they will grow away well and improve in colour instead of losing it as would happen if allowed out in all weathers.

Separating the Sexes. They need not have such early attention in weeding out as with the lighter breeds, which are far more precocious than the Sussex, 14 to 16 weeks is quite soon enough to put the chicks away by themselves, and all the "crooks" can then be used for the table.

CHAPTER VIII.

THE ORIGIN OF THE LIGHTS.

I feel that this chapter will be of more than ordinary interest to the lover of the Light Sussex, for I do not remember ever seeing even a ''note'' on the above subject. The origin of the Lights, and I have good reason to know why there has never been anything penned with regard to this matter, because nothing is known about it. I must now go back to some of our first meetings before the Club was formed, and I have mentioned in a previous chapter that some of the poultry breeders of that day were very enthusiastic with regard to the Spangled, or as we have called it, the Speckled Sussex, but for the Lights they had never a good word to say, and the opposition that I and a few supporters had at times was very great, and it must be remembered that I am writing of the time when the Club was on the point of formation, and some of those who were forming it were ''Fanciers'' who had never bred a bird in their lives, in fact, I well know that at some of the meetings only two breeders were present, so this will explain to some extent the difficulties one had to overcome. One breeder was particularly angry when the question of the Light arose, because he had, and was, breeding Speckleds, and in those days had some very good birds, it was this man who tried hard—very hard—to keep the Club to only one variety, and that the Speckled, and as I have before mentioned, our dear old friend, Mr. E. J. Wadman, was ''up against'' this ''fanatic'' with the Reds, which, by the way, did

Opposition to the Lights.

not "upset" our friend so much as the Light. I well know at times it seemed like the "Red rag to the bull" if the Lights were mentioned. On every occasion of a meeting being held, the main point at issue was "A Speckled Sussex Club," and on every occasion I was "out" for a Variety Club, with, of course, the Lights included. I had bred these birds for years, and well knew they were a variety on their own, just as much as were the Speckled and the Reds. I knew they could be bred to type and colour, and also knew what a valuable bird they would be as an all round fowl— but our "Speckled Friend" would not have it, and said there was no such thing as a White Sussex—for in those days the term was "White," not "Light," which, of course, was wrong, they could not be a "White" owing to the black in flights' tail and hackle. Well, matters became more tangled, and at one meeting Delegates to (and we used to meet several times in a month), I Heathfield. suggested forming a sub-committee and arranging a trip to the Heathfield fattening sheds to show the "un-believers" that there were as many Lights in the fattening coops as Speckled ; and on this point I got my proposition carried, with the result that I made arrangements with some of the largest fatteners to take a party of delegates down and go through the sheds (not an easy trip to arrange, for in those days the Heathfield fatteners were very reticent and adverse to any stranger coming into their domains). However, I was very well known, and I soon had matters fixed up. I may say right here, that I had gone a little further than arranging to take the delegates over the sheds— I had made a special effort to see that these sheds had a goodly number of Light—or White, as they were called in the pens. It may even be that the other colours, especially the Speckled, had been put away in the dark, for, really, there were surprisingly few Speckled to be

seen, and the astonishment of the faces of our "Speckled
Members" was great, and to one or two of those who
were in "the know," it was a very amusing part of
our visit. The further we went the less Speckled did
we find—a fair amount of Reds, but hundreds of Lights—
and when I say hundreds, it means many, for some
of these fatteners would have 4 to 6,000 chickens up in
the fattening pens at one time. Lights, Lights, every-
where, and on chatting to the owners or the crammers,
I asked which class of bird they found fatten out best,
and which put on flesh the quickest. All and every
man said : "Oh, guvenor, give us the Whites ; they
be the chicks for us. We can get 'em fed up and on the
market quicker than anything else we've got 'ere."
(It almost seemed that some of these men had been
"primed," the manner and quick way they "rapped"
out these remarks, especially as the Sussex crammer

Chicken in
the Fattening
Sheds. is not usually a fast-speaking individual). We went
through alley-way after alley-way full of chickens,
thousands of them, and ranged on both sides as one
walked down the lines, a pathway being made of old
"railway sleepers," where the pens were out of doors,
and at this particular farm most of them *were* placed
outside. In the shed the floors were just hard, dried
earth rammed down solid. It was truly a sight to see
all these birds up for cramming, and interested some
of our party considerably, for they had never before
seen a fattening farm, nor had they ever come into
touch with the old "Sussex Higgler." I well remember,
although it was several years ago, a surprise that one

A Sussex
Chicken killed
by a Sussex
Higgler. gentleman at least had. He asked one old chap how
long it took him to kill and pluck a bird, and as the
owner was kind enough to say any of my party could
buy a couple of fowls if they wished, it gave them an
opportunity to see the skill of the Sussex fattener at his
own job. Mr. D. Roberts, for that was the gentleman's

name, took out his watch, and I remember it was a heavy gold one, which the old man looked at with something like amaze, and as he was asked how long it would take him to kill and pluck, he said : "Oh ! I dunno; not long, I reckon." I said : "But, man, you know how long, don't you ? How many years have you been at this work ?" "Oh !" says he, "nigh on forty-six year come dis spring. So I've had a few 'underd duzon through my 'ands in dat time, ain't I ?" (They always speak of them as so many hundred dozen when putting up in the fattening pens.) Well, the old chap opened a pen, and was on the point of picking out a brownish-coloured chicken, but when I saw him doing this I stopped him, saying, "No; get out one of the White Sussex. I want these gentlemen to see how this kind of bird 'kills out.' " And so he took out and The Old Man killed what to some of the delegates was the first Light Timed. Sussex chicken they had ever seen, and, timed by the repeater from the moment of putting his hand in the pen and taking the bird out to be killed, plucked and rough stubbed, the time taken was three minutes twenty-seven seconds, and the amusing part of this demonstration was the bird's muscular movements had not ceased when the old chap had finished, and the quaint look of astonishment on his face when told he'd only been those few minutes, for to him it was nothing wonderful, he was doing this work mechanically, as it were, every three days per week, for killing days were three a week and always regular. We saw on the A Cuckoo occasion of this visit, too, several of those "cuckoo" Sussex. coloured Kent and Sussex birds which I used to like so much, and if ever there is another colour of Sussex brought out, I hope it may be this colour. Although I have had for two or three years past some correspondence from one of our members in the Channel Islands, who tells me he has brought out and perfected a pure "Black" Sussex!! But should any reader have to-day some of the strain and class and type of bird I am referring to, I should be glad to hear from him, because I have bred many of them and found them to be most excellent and fast-growing chickens, and quite believe they could be bred to colour and type as any of the other varieties. I will only add that by the time we had been through the sheds and the outside "lines" of the chicken at one or two of the large fattening farms in the Heathfield district, I had convinced, and very fully, too, the party of delegates that there were Light Sussex, and a goodly number, too. In fact, the surprise to these good fellows was that there were so many more "Lights" than Speckled. The party, before they came down to the Heathfield district, thought Speckleds were the *only* colour of Sussex. Needless to say, I was quite satisfied with the trip and its results, and so, at the next meeting held it was unanimously agreed that a Club should be formed to encourage the breeding of the Light, Red or Brown, and Speckled Sussex. I will give further notes on the worthy Red or Brown in a later chapter.

CHAPTER IX

THE ORIGIN OF THE BREED.

It dates back long before my appearance, although not, of course, bred to colour as were many of the varieties, and, as will be seen from the drawing of the Kent and Sussex fowl in 1847 (with honors), they were not quite of the type at that time as we see them in the recent photographs I have taken. But this drawing proves without any doubt they were a recognised fowl as far back as "'47," and that is going further back than many popular "so-called" breeds of to-day.

I am not out to quote here from Mr. Lewis Wright's book, or anybody else's book or writings, what the Light Sussex was made up from, because I've never yet found or read a single line written by anyone who had ever bred them—the breeders of the early Sussex were farmers not writers—and on going through different "Standard works," one cannot find any breeders' remarks. But the Authors generally say, "I had to get this information, as I have never *bred* the bird." So, I say, I am out to tell you how *I* bred them, and the points I found in them. As far back as I can remember I could see flocks of white-coloured, strong-boned, hardy chicken on the farm. My people used to rear several hundreds, and in those days before much time or thought was given to treating chicken which ailed there were hundreds of chicks lost every year from "gapes," and I well remember that the "White Chicken were bred in large numbers, because they were, or seemed to be, practically immune from that treacherous

The Hardiness of the Light.

complaint. Here is a point of interest showing the hardiness of the Lights in the early days, even before it got a proper name. In those days many of the chicks were almost white throughout, a little black in the tail, but no hackle, very fast growers, and easy to rear in winter and early spring. As time went on, I got very interested in this early spring chick and began to find out something about the "mate up" of them, and to see that the largest boned, largest grown white hens were saved for breeding, and to get large—"feathered-legged in most cases"—white male birds and put down with them birds with a good dash of Brahma in them, and

Light Sussex sent to Kilkenny and Co. Wexford and Cork. sometimes Cochin (from which to-day our yellow Light colour comes), and as years passed I advertised them in Ireland as one of the fastest growing chicken for the table, and I may say that the stock from many of those birds which I sent out in the early days was the foundation of many thousands of chicken which were eventually sent into the Heathfield district for fattening

The predominating blood of the Light. purposes. The foundation of the Lights—I mean the predominating blood of this bird—was Brahma, Cochin and Dorking, S. Grey), and this is all proved by the feathers on leg and the colour of the Brahma—(I am referring to the early days), the yellow and sapphires from the Cochin, and the five toes from the Dorking. I used to get 75 per cent. of five toes at one time, and in the first few years of the Lights' existence as an Exhibition fowl many of the rather well-marked and good type chicken had to be "turned down" owing to this defect (the five toes). The hardiness of such a breed was assured. Having a considerable amount of Brahma in it, of course, made for a robust and large frame, but when I found a predominance of the Dorking in them, as sometimes would happen by using a Dorking cross cock or cockerel, I found the tendency in the chicks at 10 to 12 weeks old was to get "leggy." A form of leg weakness

would develop, the bird being too long in the leg. The
Lights in the early days were far more broody than is the Broodiness in
the Early Days
case to-day. It was a "trait" fostered more then,
owing somewhat to their value as mothers in bringing up
large broods early in the season, but also because the hens
in those times were the only means of hatching, there
being no Incubators, and so this broodiness was rather
encouraged than otherwise. And yet another point to
encourage this broodiness was found by the greater age
of the bird—they used to be kept for four or five years—
and I have even known them much older. Consequently,
with an aged flock the broody fever would be even more
persistent. However, they were all made use of as
"hatching and rearing machines."

These "White" chicken, with a touch of black Bred solely
for the
in the tail, and some with hackles, were bred solely Fattening Pens
for the "fattening coops." They had the qualities,
they were easy to rear, and consequently there were
fewer cases of mortality, and people soon found that
"they *suited* the place," hence more and more "Whites"
could be seen as years went on. It was just a case of the
survival of the fittest, and, as we all know, the Lights
are a very hardy, strong bird, so they won their way
through by their good qualities, and, in my opinion,
nothing could have been a greater recommendation.
I am quite sure, too, they have kept up their reputation
in the show pens.

The feather on leg was troublesome during the Breeding out
the feathers
first few years of breeding to standard, and I have seen on leg.
many Lights thrown in the first days of exhibition
with considerable leg feathering, and the judge having
to give away to it, because very few birds in the class
would be quite free. And, "just a whisper," those
which had no feather on the legs often had an appearance
of being recently entangled in barbed wire, and, on
looking fairly closely at the birds' legs, "small holes"

could be seen and congealed blood. I have many times seen this at the early shows, but I'm not actually stating here that the feathers *were* pulled out. Oh ! no. It may be, as I've said, they had unfortunately got caught up in some barbed wire. For, of course, people who had never before put birds into a show would not know how to "trim and fake." I understand it is only *old* hands who try that sort of thing.

Breeding out the fifth toe, Another disagreeable little trait the Lights would have If an extra good chick was hatched and reared, and he had the most promising type and showed good colour and was free from leg feathering, just out of pure cussedness that chick would carry the fifth toe, and so not qualify for showing. There was much discontent about the fifth toe being "cut off." Many people thought it should be left, yet it was useless, and a breed which carries five toes is not too easy to rear on heavy land. Again, it has not been difficult to cut it out, for to-day it is very rare to see a bird with five toes.

Breeding to Colour. From the first it has been found difficult to get the colour just as it should be, and so it is with any fowl. They are not so easy to breed as some would like to imagine. I am writing this chapter in March, 1920, and where to-day can we find a perfect Light Sussex chicken or cockerel ? I admit—and I am sure my readers will do so too—that we have made See S.C.S. Sussex Cockerel, 1904. great headway since I showed my Light Sussex Cockerel at the Park Royal Show in 1904. Just look well at that photo, and then turn over to Light Sussex cockerel, 1920. This is good proof of what has been done, but I say again, we haven't a perfect cock or cockerel in the country to-day, and there are some "dismal White backs in the Cockerels. Jimmies" who say we shall never breed a white-backed cock or cockerel ; we can get them white in the pullets and hens, but not in cocks or cockerels. We have seen one or two at the larger shows during the past

A FINE GROUP OF EARLY HATCHED LIGHT SUSSEX.

SHOWING THE TYPE OF THE "SUSSEX" IN 1847.

LIGHT SUSSEX COCKEREL.
1st Royal, 1904.

LIGHT SUSSEX PULLET.
1st Royal, 1904

RED SUSSEX PULLET.
1st Royal, 1904.

LIGHT SUSSEX PULLET SHOWING LONG BACK.

SOME PROMISING 1920 LIGHT SUSSEX.

FEATHERS FROM NECK HACKLE OF LIGHT SUSSEX.

Incorrect, showing too much black   Correct, showing black centre with
also white shafting.   white edge.

year or so getting nearer to the white top colour, but even these would not bear close inspection. Yet, I say, "in time" we shall do it, and I think it shows great skill and great patience to get the birds up to the standard to-day from the rough material we started with as shown in 1904.

To-day we see cockerels put into the breeding pen with dark hackles—very well defined hackles—but sooty or even black under colour. This may be all very well to breed pullets, but the percentage of fair male birds from such a mated pen would be small, if any. Most of our Club members know my views upon dark under colour. I have for years very strongly advocated "white to the flesh," and have proved beyond doubt it has been, and is being, bred. Yet there are some who will continue to say it's an impossibility to breed a bird with a good hackle and yet get a clear under colour. I say there is no such word as "impossible." No, that kind of word I do not know. We can breed a bird white to the flesh, and I have taken photos recently of such birds, and with hackles as nearly perfect as we want them; also flight and tail feathers right.

This is the colour that worries me more than under-colour. Top colour in the male birds. Yes, this is indeed a problem at the moment. We have got the points of the bird well in hand; we have got good hackles; we have got good tails, good face, and the combs far better than they were a few years since, but we still have that yellow back, those feathers still tinged with yellow; and on some farms every bird that is mated in the pens this season shows a strong yellow colouring. To those who are breeding Lights, and have a few promising cockerels, I would here give a hint which may be of value. We hear some of the old breeders say: "Oh! that yellow top;

Cockerels with Black Under Colour.

Dark Under-Colour.

Sappiness in the Light Cockerels.

How to Check Sappiness.

D

oh, that's nothing ; just caused by the sun, you know. The bird was white and quite all right last spring before he was mated, and when he is put up into the training pen he will lose that little 'sappiness' and show all right.'' I admit there is something in ''weather,'' but I also know it does not play quite such an important part, and once the yellow is ''there'' it will never come out. This I know, however, that the most promising cockerels should be placed in shaded cockerel pens or runs, and they should be reared along during spring and summer without coming into contact with sun, wind or rain. Yes, here's the point ; the wind and rain will bring out sappiness as well as sun, and many of the birds shown to-day would have very little yellow discernible if they had been treated in this way.

The Size of the Cockerels. It has often been mentioned to me that in breeding the Lights for exhibition we should lose in size and weight. This, however, is just the reverse from the case. We only have to remember the last Club Show, November, 1919, when many of the cocks and cockerels were said to be as large as turkeys, and it was one of the ''wonders'' of that great event—the tremendous size of the birds. .

Do not Sacrifice Colour for Size or weight So it has been really a case of improving size and weight, and I hope this will always be a strong point with all breeders, to keep foremost the value of size and weight. I must say that I *do* sometimes see pens of Lights mated with a small-boned and small-framed cockerel. It may be, and often is, I think, a case of late hatching— a thing we should all keep away from. It is wrong— very wrong—especially with a heavy breed as the Light Sussex.

Long and Deep. We can see by the photographs the improvements made since 1904 in length of back and size of the birds : the photograph taken a few days since shows a bird nearly twice the size of my Royal winner, 1904. Long back, that's the ''line'' to keep in one's mind when mating the pen—a long back, with corresponding long breast—which really means a fine table bird with a predominence of breast flesh. That's just it, and it's where the Light Sussex stores. An ideal exhibition bird, a fine bird to the eye, handsome and yet excellent for table and good for eggs. Where can we say these things of the breeds put up in the show pens ? There is breed after breed that is absolutely useless for either eggs or table, that is grown *only* for the "eye," but in our Sussex we have all the qualities combined, and so its usefulness should appeal to the utilitarian as well as the fancier, and, unlike so many exhibition breeds, the "culls" are of value for the fattening pen of cockerels, and pullets can be run on for egg production.

The Ideal. Exhibition and Utility Combined.

CHAPTER X.

THE LIGHT SUSSEX HEN OR PULLET.

Photo 1904
Winner S.C.S.
Here we have a photograph of my first, at the
Park Royal, 1904. Look at the lop-sided thing; no
shape, no carriage, no colour. What a picture! Yet
she was the best of her kind at the show, and she has
one redeeming feature. Note the length of back.
Yes, I'd get that in all my Lights, the one great point
which we have "stuck" to during the breeding up of
the Sussex. She had a fair hackle, too, for a Light
in those days, and she was not long in the legs. So,
to sum up, she had several points in her favour, if
looked into closely, and I'm afraid one wanted a good
Photo Light
Sussex
Pullet, No. 1.
pair of well-focussed spectacles to get *all* those points
out. Now, we will look at the photograph the other
side of the page. This is one of a Light which I took
a few days since, and if this is compared with the other,
it will give one a very good idea of what has been done
in 16 years of proper breeding, proper mating and
Building up
the Lights.
proper selection. Isn't it something for the Sussex
Club and the members of that Club to be proud of, to
be able to improve at such a rate? Or, may I say, for
the breeders to "build up" a bird as shown here from
such material as we had 16 years ago? Yes; I think
it does credit to very many breeders, lots of whom I
could mention here had I the time and space, some
whose names will appear later, and who are still carrying on the good work, and some who have passed
beyond the border, but who have left a good name
behind and have seen the "spade" work of the Club.

LIGHT SUSSEX HEN.

The pullets are easier to breed than the cockerels; The Colours of the Pullets. that is usually so, and will always be seen in classes at the large shows by the heavy entry of pullets against cockerels. In passing, I must mention the heavy entry of pullets in the last Club Show, November, 1919, of which I will have more to say in a later chapter; no fewer than 53 birds being entered in the Light pullet class at this event. No little matter for a Judge to get his winners. He had to take both time and patience, but more of this anon. The pullet shown in A pure White Under-Colour. the photograph has a good hackle—a well defined hackle—a good tail with about the proper amount of black in it, and plenty of black in the flights. Yet, when I pulled back the top colour on the back, I could see white feathers right down to the skin, and yet we are sometimes, nay, I might say, often, told it is not possible to breed a pullet perfectly white in the back and carrying a good hackle. It is. I say it is, and is being done every day, and we must "go" for it. We must be more strict upon this point in the show pen. There must not be much given away. It should be a very strong point with all judges. And yet I have seen at quite recent shows—shows late in 1919—where even sooty top colour birds have been awarded honours. Note the revised standard I have published, and tell your judges to note it too. We have had many, many hours over those standards. None know or realize that fact greater than I, and so I say let us adjudicate accordingly to that standard to the letter or scrap the "Or Scrap the Standard." rule of standard and each man go on his own. It would then be a case something like every person ordering their own "weather"—a general mix up. To-day there is too much "laxity" allowed, and it's a case of "pulling" the lines in a little more, and while on this subject, a question raised recently by Mr. Clem Watson, a club judge, on the "pulling of feathers," which has "Pulling the Feathers."

been noticed during the past year. It is quite right that this kind of thing should be stopped, and a firm hand must be placed upon such practices. In mentioning this matter, it reminds and brings me back to the early days of showing the Sussex. If we had "pulled" unsightly feathers from our birds in those days, I am very well sure most of them by the time we had finished would not have had more than half-a-dozen feathers left, and it would have been impossible for the judge to know if the bird was a Speckled, Light or Red. Let us see to it that all this kind of thing is dealt with as it should be by all whose duty it is to adjudicate.

The Face and Comb.   I am glad to say, as years go on, we find an improvement in the face and in the comb of the Lights. For several years very little notice was taken of the comb in shows. I think this was mainly due to their being so many other more important points to note and to breed for the birds that the comb was hardly given a thought. But to-day we do certainly see more care given to it, and *Side Sprigs.* rightly so. I have many times seen birds winning and taking firsts and specials with combs showing large side sprigs. Now this is going a little too far. Here, again, the Standard should be adhered too, and yet has often been entirely ignored. In some of the chicks, too, the combs have been far too large, and in some dropping over on one side. We do not want a large comb in the Sussex, and we should try to get the comb well and evenly *The Neck Hackle.* serrated. A question often put by one who is taking up the breeding of the Lights is, "How do you define the neck hackle? Should it be black, or white? I can never understand quite what is wanted." Now, the standard needs : "Neck Hackle," White Striped with black. So the beginner should get into his mind white, not black. The white should predominate, or I ought *How the Feathers should be Marked.* perhaps to say, be the predominating colour—a white feather with a black centre That's it. That is what we have to go for, and not a black feather striped with white, as so many people who first take up the breed seem to think. The hackle, in my opinion, is the part of colouring which makes the Lights such a handsome bird, and is a point which should always have consideration when making up a pen or buying in a flock. Hens with weak hackle are generally said to be free from any sootiness or dark under colour, but this is not always the rule; in fact, by no means so. However, if one has a mob of hens with weak hackles, then the male bird should have a heavy hackle, and even if dark in under colour, will often throw some perfect-coloured chicks. *Mating for Hackle.*

We sometimes see birds in the show pen with this defect. It goes without saying, a bird with white on Lobes should be passed, but I have at times seen this ignored. One should not breed from a cockerel with this defect, for it is generally seen in the progeny if used for mating. However, should this particular cockerel be of extra good type and otherwise sound, it could be used for a pullet pen and would throw pullets true and free from the defect. *White in Lobes*

A cockerel or hen with a wiry tail or crooked back should never be used in the breeding pen, however good they may be in colour. Also, a bird should be discarded if she has a crooked breast bone. I do not mean just a slight crook which one often sees, and which is caused more generally by the bird being allowed to perch while too young. Such a slight crook as this is of no harm and not "bred in," but where it is a decidedly "curved" breast bone this points to heredity, and such a bird should be kept out of the breeding pen. *Wiry Tail*

It is perhaps not too generally known that the Lights are easily acclimatised, and so are most suitable to send abroad, even to a hot climate. For years past I have exported many Lights, and to all parts of the world, even South India and Central Africa. Yet, in all *The Lights for Export.*

cases, do I get a very good report, the birds settling down soon and well, and apparently little the worse for a long and trying voyage or the high temperatures or variation of temperature as the case may be. Therefore, the Lights can be highly recommended for export purposes.

Leggy as Chicken.
The cockerels are inclined to legginess as chickens, and a word here I would like to say, more especially to those who buy eggs of the Lights for the first time, for mating purposes. As the chicks grow they are inclined to become leggy, and some breeders are frightened when they see this, and think the chicks will be of no use. Personally, I like to see a young Light Sussex Chick at 12 to 16 weeks old on the "long leg side." Such a bird will most often "come down," and when finished to a fine shaped bird, and if he is close and "down on the ground" at this age, he often turns out too short in leg, which is a fault too. So to those who are beginnners with rearing the breed let me say, it they watch the "leggy" cockerel they will generally have cause to be pleased with them later.

Much more could I write on the good qualities of the Lights, and of their great value as an all round, general purpose fowl, but I've the other varieties to deal with, and must therefore conclude the chapter on the Lights by saying they can be highly recommended to every lover of poultry, for their beauty, for their egg laying proclivities, and for their table properties, and I again
Last Words of Praise of the Lights.
say that it is very few exhibition fowls indeed that have so many good and useful points. I hope to see the day when the Light Sussex is the most popular and the largest bred fowl in the world, and when it holds this great position I have sufficient faith in it to say that it will "keep at the top" when it gets there.

RED SUSSEX COCK.

CHAPTER XI.

THE RED SUSSEX.

I next take the Reds. What do these come from ? An all-round Fowl. How were they bred ? And what are they like in comparison with the other varieties ? As an all-round bird they are like the other Sussex ; they are good and most excellent for the fattening crate, making healthy birds for table at an early age.

As I mentioned in a previous chapter, the Reds were not easy to standardise, owing to the "Jealousy" of the "Spangled" Breeders, and although they did not have the same opposition as the Lights, and were merely "tolerated"by some of the "so-called" fanciers, yet it was difficult at first to get them recognised and to place them on a footing with the "Spangled."

We have to thank Mr. E. J. Wadman, who in those days lived at Hurst Barns, East Chiltington, and who gave up so much time to attend meetings and "back" up the Reds, although a large farmer, who could ill afford to spare the time. He also helped to swell the entries at the first Club Show, and I can go further still, and say he formed one of the party who went to the first Club Show at Park Royal to see the birds penned, and Mr. E. J. Wadman was rewarded by winning a first and special, the latter being the first silver medal presented by the Club. Now, when we first made up the standard we called them Reds, Red or Brown, and I've said many Red or Brown. times if we had left it at this and made "*Black in Breast admissible,*" we should to-day be breeding a far more useful bird without the introduction of the "Browns"

at all. The class of bird I knew in those days as a **Red**
was quite different to the bird of to-day. I am not
"out" to say we have not got a useful bird in the present
day Red, but we have not got what we "*Might have had*"
had men known more about a table fowl when the Red
Standard was brought out. The Red of that day was a
mixture in colour and size of the present day Red *and*
Brown Sussex, and there we should have left it, and as a
matter of fact, did do so for the first few years.

Reds shown
with Black
Breasts.

There are a few fanciers left to-day who remember
Mr. D. Roberts, of Lewes, showing a grand old Red or
Brown cock, and showing him for two or three seasons,
with quite a black breast, and this bird won all the
Silver Medals given by the Club in the Red or Brown
classes, until one after the other pointed out that the
bird was not true to colour and the Press took the
matter up—I have cuttings by me now—and in due
course the standard was altered and the heading of
colour more clearly defined, and the old black-breasted
cock had to take a back seat.   I say he should have been
allowed to stay, and had this been so we should only
to-day have had the three breeds or varieties of Sussex,
and which, in my opinion, would have been far better.

THE OLD "RED" BIRD.

Since writing this Chapter I have received the
following from Mr. David Roberts :—"Your memory
for facts are simply remarkable, and I have read it
through several times and I do not think I can improve
on it.

There is one point I might mention, and that is the
one fact of refusing good money for a bird, and then in
a day or two to lose the bird or 101 things happening.
In my case I refused over £20 for mine on the Monday,
and on the Tuesday night I went to lock the shed up
for the night, and, unknown to myself, locked a cat up
with the bird. Unlocking the door next morning the

cat rushed out before the door was well open and I walked in to find the bird *dead*, probably they had fought each other and the cat got the best of it.''

Not that, now we've got them, I am going to ''cut'' the ''Brown''—they are good and useful, and I am giving them a chapter later on. But we *had* the bird once and, owing to a few ''cranks'' in the Club, lost it. I bred some Reds which took first and reserve at the first Club Show, and the hens were of large type and long back, but in those early days the hens were not so good as the cockerels, and the breasts were a very light colour, as indeed were many of the hens right through. This was often seen quite a buff colour, and it was only by ''shouting'' we got the deeper ''Sussex Red.'' I used to write quite a lot about the Reds in those days, and was always ''going'' for a *deep dark red* like the Red Sussex Cattle. That was the colour I wanted to see, and at the last Club Show held in November, 1919, we did see the colour, too. We have to-day the proper Red Sussex cattle colour, and it's very handsome too. The hens have it as well as the cocks, and I see it in the two and three-year-old birds, too, so showing it has come to stay and does not fade away. The Reds are easier to keep to colour than the Lights and Speckleds, although, like most exhibition birds, it is wise to give them shelter and shade, and by keeping them from sun, rain and wind, the colour will be much improved and will be more lasting. At one time I thought the size of the Reds was going down, but the last Club Show put up some excellent specimens, with length of back and depth of breast, which is so necessary in all the colours of the ''Sussex.'' A Red Sussex cockerel will always weigh more than at first sight one may judge. The Reds are closer of feather than the Light; there is more game blood in them, and a well-bred Red will carry a fine lot of breast flesh. I should like to see

Reds in 1903.

Red Sussex Cattle Colour.

The Colour does not Fade.

Size of Reds.

The Reds as Table Birds.

more breeders take up the Red, and I think it is due to little knowledge of the variety in many cases that it has lagged behind somewhat in popularity. If people knew what a fine table bird the Red is they would "go" for it and breed more. Its hardiness, too, is in its favour for winter and early spring rearing, although as a winter layer it is not so good as the Light. Here, again, the game blood has something to do with it.

A Good
Sitter.

The Red is a reliable "broody," and will cover and hatch a good batch of eggs. I have many times put 17 eggs under a Red in the early spring and made up the brood when hatched to 20 chicks, and the Reds will take them all and bring them up as easily as some breeds will manage a dozen. They seldom give any trouble during the hatching period, and I have often said that half-a-dozen Red pullets or hens are worth an incubator any day when they become broody.

RED SUSSEX HEN.

CHAPTER XII.

THE ORIGIN OF THE REDS.

We can go back many years with the Reds, and I have matter before me saying the old Red Dorking or Kent ^{Black in Breast,} or Sussex fowl was bred extensively in many forms for "table chicken." They had the three white tibbs. As I have mentioned elsewhere, the Reds should have been black-breasted, and we should to-day have had the Red and the Brown in one. The best cocks were bred with black in the breast; the hens were a deeper red when mated with the black-breasted cocks, and in the first few years of exhibition they had black, and in some cases nearly all black winning.

This brings me to the "make up of the breed," ^{Black Breasted Game.} which was formed up mainly from the old dark Dorking and black breasted game, hence my reason again explained for the black in breast. The type, too, of the old Dorking can well be seen in our present-day Red where bred for type and size. I am not quoting the "standards" as I take each variety of Sussex, as I may deal with it all in a special chapter, but I cannot let the Reds pass without referring to the standard.

"GENERAL CHARACTERISTICS OF HEN."

"*Plumage*" *Close.*—Now, according to standard, ^{Close feather.} this applies to all the four varieties of "Sussex," and is hardly fair, because I say in the Reds it is naturally a close-feathered bird—I might almost use the term "hard" feather—and I think in our standard we should have been right to give the Red this distinction.

A Deep Red.   As will be seen by my coloured plate, the Reds of to-day have the deep red body colour, and this is correct. In the early days it was the exception rather than the rule to see this nice deep "Sussex Cattle" Red, but I am glad to see to-day most of the pens shows this beautiful colour. There is to-day a red plumaged

The Red a Handsome Fowl.   bird in the country which is very popular, and when put up and compared with the Red Sussex there is no comparison. The Red Sussex will beat it "hollow" on several points, and I am thinking that had the Red Sussex been given the "booming" that the other breed mentioned has had, to-day our "Red" would have been the favourite breed. Take, for instance, one

Colour of Flesh and Legs.   point of the Red Sussex as a fine class table bird, and, after all, those are really the points that mostly "tell." The Reds have a nice white leg, and the flesh is of a beautiful white, fine in grain and texture. Now turn to the other breed, and you get a "yellow" leg and consequently yellow flesh, and yet that bird is bred more extensively to-day, just because our "Red" has not been "pushed" so much. However, my opinion is that the best will eventually come into its own, and I believe there is a big future for the Red Sussex in this and other countries, and when the "time" comes, there

Size of Egg.   will not be enough to go round." The Reds lay a large egg, and is nearly always well over 2 ozs., They

Winter Layers.   lay well in the early part of the season, and it has always been shown that they are good winter layers by the number of early chicks which could be bred from them by the "chicken farmers."

Neck Hackle.   How few we see in the show pen with a good hackle ; in fact, we often cannot see a hackle at all, yet the "Standard" says : "Neck hackle, rich dark red

striped with black," and this in both the cock and hen.
I am of opinion that the hackle has been too lightly
gone over by the Judges in the past ; they seem to have
"left it" out ; forgotten it—and the result has been
that the breeders have not thought it worth while to
bother about trying to breed for a striped neck hackle.
Now, I say if the standard of excellence puts down the
"line" to breed a neck hackle then this should be done Breed for a Good Neck Hackle
—or leave it out of the standard of excellence—it must,
or should be, one or the other. The few birds
which have been bred with a neck hackle certainly
have a very handsome appearance, and I do think that
this should be given all the possible encouragement.
The coloured plate of the Red I am showing here will
give some idea of the improvement in a Red when the
neck hackle is well defined.

When mating a pen of Reds keep in mind that Keep Size Foremost
size is required, and do not sacrifice too much for other
points and so neglect size; the cock should be large and
upstanding, not leggy, but, again, not short on the
leg. We do not want to see them too low or they give
out the appearance of an Orpington. The width of Wide Chest.
the chest, too, in the male should form a strong feature.
We see far too many birds in the show pen with narrow
breasts, and this narrowness should be more stringently
dealt with. All the four varieties of Sussex should have
very great depth and width of chest, and to everyone
who is breeding the Sussex let me make this quite plain,
and let it be understood by everyone that it is a very
important point in breeding the Sussex.

I have previously mentioned that the Red Sussex Red Legs
is white in leg colour, but yet we often see birds shown
with very red legs. I have often had the question put :
What is the cause of the red leg developing ? Well, it
is not far to seek. If the bird is in a large run, or is
mated, the legs will quickly become red in colour, but

if the bird is put into a training pen, on clean straw or litter, or put into a cockerel house with an open small wire pen attached, the legs will keep a white colour.

Breed More Reds. During the last few years more Reds have been exported, and chiefly to the States, although this is not their favourite breed. I should like to see many more Red Sussex bred and the variety made far more popular, for it is a handsome bird, in addition to being an excellent table fowl. I can safely recommend it to any and all who want a high-class breed of poultry.

LIGHT SUSSEX COCKEREL.

RED SUSSEX COCKEREL.

RED SUSSEX PULLET.
Winner Club Show, 1919.

SPECKLED SUSSEX COCK.
Club Show Winner, 1919.

Showing dark blotches. Clear dark mahogany with white tips.

SPECKLED SUSSEX PULLET.
Club Show Winner, 1919.

A SPECKLED PULLET
A Winner in 1919.

A GOOD SPECKLED SUSSEX COCKEREL.
With long back.

SPECKLED SUSSEX COCK.

CHAPTER XIII.

THE SPECKLED SUSSEX.

Here we have the oldest of the Sussex family, called by many names, amongst them the Old Kent Spangled, the Old Barnyard Spangled, the Old Spangled Sussex, and later on we find it described as the Old Spangled Dorking, and so on until we come down to the day of Spangled Sussex, and then to the Speckled Sussex. The bird of the old days was quite a different colour and type of to-day—type it certainly had in those days (of a kind), and several years before the Sussex Club was formed I got into touch with breeders in the Counties of Kent, Surrey and Sussex (I could find no other County where they were bred) ; and on making much inquiry, found in the majority of cases the Old Spangled had been bred on the farms as far back as these people could remember. I well know I had the breed quite distinct as from a lad, and so it went forth in the days of the formation of the Club that the Speckled was the only Sussex bird which could be named. with such results as our readers now know. We had a great many meetings at which the points of the Speckled were discussed, but never a question as to whether it should form a variety on its own as with the Lights and Reds. No, it was unanimously decided to have a Club for the Speckled if for nothing else. I would like here to mention a few of the oldest breeders of these handsome Sussex, although in those days not so pretty as at the present time. The late Mr. John Ade, then living at Wilmington, Sussex, was an old breeder of

E

Wilmington
Sussex.

the Speckled, and it was in that district (under those beautiful downs, with the Giant, The Wilmington Giant, which many, many years ago was carved out in the Chalk of the Downs, holding a staff in each hand, and a landmark for many miles, also could be seen from the trains passing between Berwick and Polegate, looking down), that I found more Speckled Sussex than

The First
Royal Show
Winner.

at any part of East Sussex, and it was here that the first Speckled Hen won first prize and medal at the Royal Agricultural Show in 1904. She was bred at Wilmington, and shown by Mr. Charles Page, long since "gone out" of poultry keeping. This bird I judged at a local show which I organised after a course of lectures given at Wilmington School in 1901, and we had classes for Speckled. I well remember the many different colours shown there, and some useful types amongst them, but this particular hen (pullet in that year) was a heavy, but short-backed type, also short in the leg, much shorter than we breed them to-day; the back too would not "pass" to-day. However, she was a fine bird for her time, and the best, according to the judge, which was put up at the Royal.

The Lewes
Fanciers.

At the Lewes Fanciers' Show held in November 1903, classes for Sussex were put up, and the Speckled filled fairly well—a breeder, who then lived at Buxted, Sussex, Mr. G. J. Lenny, being the fortunate winner; in fact, he carried off most of the prizes and honours. He was an old fancier and could put the birds up in better condition than most people of that day, and he was breeding a very large type of Speckled. There were many of them very long on the leg, but far better

Caponized
Speckleds.

in type and also in colour than the Wilmington hen. Mr. Lenny was then at that time the largest breeder of Speckleds, and believed in no other breed; he used to have the young cockerels caponized, and I have seen, on going through his pens, several nice young Speckled

Cockerels weighing 8 or 9 lbs. each, in large coops on the ground brooding and "mothering" a large batch of young chicks. So we can say this is another point in favour of the Speckleds; and it cannot be said for many of the present day exhibition fowls that the male birds made good mothers. There used, years ago, to be many birds caponized in East Sussex, but to-day we see very few. I have treated Brahmas in this way, and used them as the Speckled Sussex—as fosters—to bring up large broods of chicken, and they will carry out the work like a good old hen, and can be always relied upon to cover the chicks well and look after them as well, and, perhaps, better than their own mothers.

Speckled Cockerels as Mothers.

The Speckled Sussex soon gained favours from the public when seen in the show pen, and for a time were by far the most popular. They were taken up by breeders of other varieties and soon began to spread to all parts of England. Ireland had had them years before the Club was formed, and I have seen them sent over to Uckfield in the large Irish crates, and in those days stuffed to "the overflowing" with birds, many of them being crushed on the journey. I have seen Speckled of all colours and all types, yet many of them even then coming pretty true to markings and level in colours. I have seen, too, in the early shows, Speckled Sussex hens and pullets varying from light fawn ground colour to almost jet black. Some would be covered with large white spots and splashes of black, with little or no brown, and in the next pen we would see a light brown ground work with hundreds of tiny little white spots and no black at all. The cockerels would have no even markings except upon the breast, and the tail and flight feathers would be quite white, so from this one can gather what a variety of colours could be seen at some of the first shows where classes for the Sussex were put up.

Various Colours of Speckled.

CHAPTER XIV.

THE SPECKLED OF TO-DAY.

The Speckled
as it is To-day.

I may say that of all the four varieties of the Sussex none have made greater improvement in colour than the Speckled. Even during the last two years they have become more clearly defined, and much of the improvement is due to one of our largest and best known breeders of to-day, Mr. A. J. Falkenstein. Here is a breeder who knows how to mate the birds ; he knows what he is "out" for when he puts up a pen, and I am quite sure that much thanks is due to Mr. A. J. Falkenstein for keeping the breed going during the War, and also for advancing the colour in the Speckleds.

Rich Dark
Mahogany.

The very "word" sounds nice — rich, dark mahogany ! Yes, that's the ground colour, and until the last Club Show—1919—was seldom seen, and it is for this that so much is due to Mr. Falkenstein's mating and breeding. He has bred the birds and shown them to the public, and although there has been criticism, it is proved beyond doubt that the colour is right— rich, dark mahogany. It's a fine colour, and a cockerel or a pullet carrying this colour is beautiful to look upon.

The
Standard of
Colours for
the
Speckled.

It is only recently the wording for the standard of colour has been revised, and what we have to be thankful for is that the Speckled has been bred to this dark rich colour before the standard "asked for it." The bird has been so bred and shown to the public, and, of course, much admired, and now the standard of colour reads aright, and although this revised standard does not come into force until next year—1921—yet there are to-day many pens mated which will throw some birds coming up to the new standard of colour.

SPECKLED SUSSEX HEN.

In the old standard for colour of neck hackle of
the Speckled Sussex, it reads :—Head and neck hackle,
reddish brown, striped with black. To-day, the
standard reads :—Head and neck hackle, rich, dark
mahogany striped with black and tipped with white.
Now, in that wording you have it clearly defined;
before, no one could quite make out what was wanted.
To-day, the standards are readable, and that is why
I have always said we should have taken three years
instead of three months to get out the standard. Perhaps
it is not quite correct even yet, but I do know it is far
more understandable, and to the novice should not now
present too many difficulties in giving a ''line of fire''
for mating up a pen of birds.

Here, again, the remainder of plumage is put in the
revised standard very plain and clear—in the old Remainder of
standard it read as—in cock, rich reddish brown, striped Plumage.
with black and tipped with white—to-day it reads—rich
dark mahogany, each feather tipped with a small white
spot, a narrow glossy black bar dividing the white from
the remainder of the feather and showing the three
colours distinctly, neither of the colours to run into
each other, under colour slate and red with a minimum
of white. Notice the clear definition here; it tells one Definition.
just what the colour should be. bred in the male bird.
Now here we have the old standard for hens. Remainder of plumage—brown, white, and black, as
evenly speckled as possible. It now reads — Head,
neck, and body colour—ground colour rich dark mahogany, each feather tipped with a small white spot, a
narrow glossy bar dividing the white from the remainder of the feather. ''The mahogany part of feather to
be free from pepperiness''—neither of the colours to ''Note''
run into each other and to shew the three colours dis- Pepperiness.
tinctly, under colour slate and red with a minimum of
white. Here again we have the body colour ''worked

out to a point,'' and anyone taking up the standard
to-day should have no difficulty in arriving at a decision
as to what the proper colouring of the Speckled should be
Such was hardly the case, however, with the old standards, and I again say that the Club has much to thank
Mr. A. J. Falkenstein for this alteration and for breeding
such a bird, and thus showing intending breeders what
a really good speckled Sussex should be like. I have
dealt rather fully with this colouring of the Speckled,
because I have felt it to be a very important point.
I have been through these standards with these several
alterations since 1903, and have never before seen it
so clearly ''brought out'' as to-day, and by analysing
the colouring as I have done in this chapter it will be
of some help and assistance, perhaps, to those who may
be taking up the breeding of the Speckled, for the first
time.

CHAPTER XV.

On looking at any of the first photographs taken Shape of Speckled. of the Speckled some years ago, we find the Speckled, especially the males, inclined to a short back, and I well know that when breeding them myself as table chicken, these were rather on the short side, although very deep on the breast. To-day we have altered all this. Note the photo of Speckled pullet which I took only a few days since. See the length of backbone and also the fine shape and fine type of the bird. Yes, the improvement in shape has been rapid during the past two years, and they are very much finer specimens than they used to be. The colour of the leg in the Speckled has improved Leg Colour. too, although I saw at the last Club Show a few that showed very red, and I do not like to see them, neither should they be "passed" so easily. It has been another Length of Leg in Speckled. difficult point to keep the leg "down" in some types, and in others they have showed tendency for "leggyness." I do not know which to be worse. Both, I will say. We certainly do not want a bird "down too much ;" for one thing, if too low she is never seen to advantage, her length will not be shown up, nor her breadth, and so we must keep away from the "low built" bird. Then, again, if we get them "leggy," this too will spoil the look of the other points, and a very good deep breasted cock or hen, when long on leg, will show on the narrow side; so, to sum up, we want birds of medium height, and this can generally be bred by giving careful thought to these special points when mating up.

Feather on Leg   We had some difficulty in the early days with slight feathers on leg, and more particularly I found this to be so with the Cockerels; now we seldom see it, but— and I'm sorry to have to write this—we often see where the feather has been, and I have more than once seen birds in a show pen having legs with "perforations," which point pretty conclusively to "leg feather pulling." I must say this is not "common," and certainly not so frequent as some years back when it was really difficult to get a good bird without this defect, for it was not so easy to breed out in the Speckleds as in the Lights, and in the Reds we seldom found any sign of leg feather,

Do not breed from a Speckled which shows Signs of Leg Feathers. owing to the different "make-up" of the variety. I will only add that it should be carefully watched, and no bird, cock or hen, should be mated if there are signs of any leg feathering, for it is a trait more easily "bred in" than" bred out."

When judging or selecting a Speckled hen for a breeding pen every care should be given to select a

Selection for Breeding Pen. bird with long, deep breast and long back. It is only by this careful selection, this careful handling, that one can hope to keep up with the standard of perfection. The "chance" mating will prove very disappointing, and it is care and thought which will give the greatest

Colour of Chicks. satisfaction during the breeding season. The colour of the chicks when first hatched are often very puzzling to the novice, and like some of our other breeds and varieties comes all sorts of colours, down to nearly black which will even sometimes turn out right. So to those who have perhaps sent away and bought a sitting or two of eggs and have paid "best pen price," when the youngsters are hatched they must be prepared for a "shock," and not to see the "rich dark mahogany," etc., etc.—that is to come later—but I have to mention these points because I know from experience there are people who think the youngsters should show at least

some of the markings of the adult bird, but such is
often not the case with young Speckled chicks. And
so by these remarks it will be seen that the chicken Weeding Out.
should not be weeded out too early. I find with this
variety it pays to keep them longer than most others,
for a cockerel will change remarkably at even 14 to 16
weeks old. The pullets can be selected sometimes
earlier, but any likely looking specimens should be
saved for a few weeks longer, and the breeder may be
rewarded by seeing a really fine coloured bird when
finished. For the benefit of the breeder who is "out" Growth of Speckled Chicks.
for table as much as for exhibition and wants quick
growing cockerels to come on for early spring, I can
say that the Speckled will not disappoint, they are very
hardy as chicken and will stand any situation or
climate ; they are not at all particular as to soil. I
have raised them on heavy clay in January, and am
able to state that leg weakness or so-called "cramp"
was a "stranger" to them ; they will grow away fast,
too, and if brought along on a good class "soft food,"
will be ready for the fattening pen at 12 weeks old, and,
in fact, they will be useful for the table at that age
if one does not want a finished bird. The skin is
white and also the flesh, and when killed and plucked
they have a very fine appearance. So, to sum up the
Speckled, I will just add that for beauty and usefulness
it is a variety of poultry difficult to beat, and, in fact,
I do not think one can ever want a better, for we must
always bear in mind that there are very few breeds of
poultry which have the combined qualities of beauty
and usefulness.

CHAPTER XVI.

THE BROWN SUSSEX.

Reds or
Browns.

I have left these over to the last, as they are the last of the varieties of "Sussex" to be drawn into the "Club," and it will be rather interesting reading if I can deal with the "bringing" out of the variety. I am quite sure in the "Browns" we have a fine class of bird for the table, and I have much to say in their favour, but I will say this yet again. Had the standard been properly fixed when we formed the Club, there would have been no Brown Sussex as known to-day, nor was there any need for a Brown. We had it in 1902 and 1903, and 1904, and so on. We had a bird which carried the two colours and qualities in one, and more especially so with the male bird. The standard said Red or Brown, and Red or Brown it should have been. I well know I did all in my power to keep it so, because I am not in favour of getting too many colours in a variety. There are far too many at the present day what I often call "side lines." They are of very little value these "Blues and Blacks," etc., etc., and when put on at shows often only get a very few entries, and I say, if we get a good variety or breed, let us rather put all our time, our thought, and our energies into the breeding and selection for improvement into that variety or breed and not "dabble" about trying to bring out a blue-black yellow or green. I know this kind of thing goes on, and I suppose always will, but I also know these "freak" varieties do not "last," so perhaps we need not worry about them. Now, my

BROWN SUSSEX COCK.

dear readers, I am not suggesting that the "Brown" is a "freak variety;" it is far from this, but I say we could have done without it, or rather would I say, we could have done without the name, for we already had the fowl. Now we've got it and taken it over to foster and to "mother," then, I say, let us breed it. Let us try and improve it and to make it known as an *Future for the Browns* ideal table bird, which to-day it is, and I am glad to write and say I believe there is a big future for the Browns. To-day they are very little known. Why at the last Dairy Show, October, 1919, there were only eight entries in the two classes for Browns; that was: four for Brown Cockerels and four for Brown Pullets. Whilst against this poor display there were 59 entries in the Light Pullets and 34 in the Light Cockerels, making a total in these two classes of 93 Lights in two classes against eight in two classes of Browns. This goes to show then how little known or how little bred the Browns are to-day. Well, I can hardly say to-day, because I have been quoting October, 1919, and to-day, April, 1920, I do know there are many more breeders who have taken up the Browns this season and are breeding them, and I believe we shall see in the show pens this coming show season some very good specimens of the Browns bred by some of the new members of the Club. I hope so—for I am very anxious to see them go—now that we have taken them up, and I have for some time said they must either be bred and taken on seriously by all breeders of the Sussex who are able to breed them, or throw them up altogether, for as they have been in the past they have been of no use to the Club or to their name; in fact, they have been a heavy loss to the Club. At the *Brown Sussex at the Club* Club Show, however, the entries improved, and the *Show, 1919,* classes filled as follows :—

Brown Cock, 6 entries; Cockerel, 9; Hen, 12;
Pullet, 12; making a total of 39 entries in the four
classes arranged for them. The colour, too, was very
good, and their size and type coming along well. This
entry, of course, goes to show there are several "Browns"
about in the country, and given a little encouragement,
we shall see them far more numerous this coming season.

HISTORY OF THE "BROWNS."

As I have before mentioned, when the Club was
first formed, the "Browns" came under the heading
of Red or Brown Sussex, but this title did not suit some
of the fanciers after two or three years of exhibition
under that name, and on 29th June, 1906, at a committee meeting held in Lewes, I read a letter from the
Secretary of the Hailsham Fanciers' Association,
asking that the word "Brown" should be struck out
and the variety to be called the Red Sussex, and it
was resolved that the matter should be put on the
agenda to be dealt with at the next annual general
meeting, and so, on the 20th December, 1906, the question
was brought forward, there being a fair number of
members present at that meeting. "It was resolved
that the word 'Brown' be omitted and that the variety
should be called the Red Sussex." So this was the
end of the first Act. There was much behind all this,
as I shall point out later. The Club now had the same
number of varieties, viz. : The Light, Red and Speckled,
and, by the way, a few months previous to this date,
one member took up a good deal of time at meetings,
etc., trying to bring on a sub-variety of Speckled Sussex
and he wanted it called "The Old Speckled Sussex."
This, however, did not meet with general approval, and
so, thank goodness, we are to-day spared from seeing
any "Old Speckled Sussex."

We now come down to the 11th June, 1908, when, Introduction of the Brown. at a meeting of the Sussex Poultry Club, I had to read the following letter from the Secretary of the Hailsham District Fanciers' Association, with reference to a resolution passed at a meeting held by their Association on the 8th May, 1908, and asking for the support of the Sussex Poultry Club :—"That this meeting of the Hailsham and District Fanciers' Association having seen the Brown Sussex fowls, introduced by Mr. John Ade, are of opinion that the Brown Sussex should be recognised as a distinct variety, and that the resolution be forwarded to the Sussex Poultry Club." There A Fourth Variety not Wanted. was some discussion on the subject, and it was soon found to be the general opinion that a fourth variety of Sussex was not wanted, and a resolution was passed to that effect, and I was instructed to write to the Secretary, stating "That the Club could not see their way to recognise the variety referred to," and so here ends Act 2, but we've more of interest to follow. The next move is on the 24th March, 1909, when a letter is read to the members of the committee of the Sussex Poultry Club from Mr. John Ade, with reference to the "*Brown Sussex,*" "being added to the present three varieties," and it was resolved to call a "Special A Special General Meeting. General Meeting to obtain the views of the members of the Club upon the matter." This Special General Meeting was held in Lewes on the 21st April, 1909, there being a very good attendance. At this meeting the late Mr. John Ade was present and made the proposition that the "Brown Sussex should be added to the three varieties fostered by the Club." There was some discussion by those present and also about thirty letters read from members who were unable to attend— most of these letters being *against* the proposition—and it was resolved "that the Club could not recognise the 'Brown Sussex.'"

Now, as the late Mr. John Ade was breeding some large framed birds of the Red or Brown colour and type, also a few others in the neighbourhood, they had
A Brown Sussex Club.
some discussion and decided to form a "Brown Sussex Club." They did this and drew up their rules, etc., and got a little Club running, holding their meetings at Hailsham, at which they had their Club Show. They also for one or two years published a "Year Book.' Naturally, such an action caused some little trouble and friction with the Sussex Poultry Club, and although, doubtless, those who formed themselves into a separate Club thought they were doing the right thing, I always felt that it was a mistake and quite running against the Mother Club; and I notice that at a meeting held by the Sussex Poultry Club on the 23rd August, 1909, the following resolution was passed :—"That the "Secretary of the Sussex Club be directed to write to "all Show Secretaries, where Sussex are supported by "the Club, with reference to the advisability of not "placing the 'Brown Sussex' immediately following "the Sussex Classes supported by this Club." The whole affair caused confusion and bother, and it was urged by many at that time that the idea was wrong, having a separate Club to run one variety on its own. And so matters went on until 1913, when it was found the Brown Sussex Club did not make headway. At
Sussex Club to take over the Browns.
a meeting held at Lewes on the 23rd October, 1913, the late Mr. John Ade brought forward the question of the "Brown Sussex," and that they be taken over by the Sussex Club, and it was decided to discuss the matter at a General Meeting to be held at the Palace Club Show; and at this meeting, held at the "Palace" on the 19th November, 1913, Mr. Ade again brought the question forward, and it was resolved, after some discussion, to refer it to the Annual General Meeting, notice to be placed on the Agenda. This brings us

down to the 10th Annual General Meeting of the Sussex Poultry Club, which was held at Lewes on the 10th December, 1913, and here the future of the Browns were finally settled, it being decided that the Club Taken over by the Sussex Club. take over the "Browns," together with the "Brown Sussex Cup," and that the "Brown Sussex Club" be dissolved. From this date the variety has at most shows had classification, but as I have pointed out in another chapter, the classes have not been well supported, and this, no doubt, is largely due to the fact that hitherto so few breeders have taken them up seriously, but I am of an opinion that they will be seen in far larger numbers at forthcoming shows, and quite rightly so, too. Let us all take up this fine class of Breed the Browns. table fowl, and let us keep in mind the size and shape of the bird. We shall find it the best table bird of the four varieties, and not at all a bad layer, certainly one of the best and quickest growing table chicken ever fostered in this country. Let us make the "Brown" better known, then. It has had a hard uphill struggle, and Hard Uphill Struggle. has been through troublesome times, but now the day has come when its great table qualities should be known by all lovers of poultry, whether it be lovers of *live* or *dead* poultry, for the Browns have a fine appearance as well as other qualities.

CHAPTER XVII.

THE "BROWNS" AS BROODIES.

I should like to mention a few points in connection with the Browns which may be useful to those who do not know or have not yet bred them. I have written of their size for table, and to some this may read that they would carry too much weight to be of much use Browns as Sitters. as a broody or sitter, but they are not in any way clumsy with their weight, and so make most excellent broodies; even as pullets they will seldom throw up their work, and being of such large frame will cover a large number of eggs. Hence, they are an ideal fowl for one to keep when they do not wish to have the trouble of working an incubator or Foster. Half-a-dozen Brown Sussex hens are better than most 100-egg Incubators and Fosters at any time, and with just ordinary management will bring off good broods and rear them, too, with very little trouble or losses. The Browns Winter Eggs take longer to come to maturity for egg production than some of the lighter framed birds, and so should be early hatched, and where this is followed out they will make excellent winter layers. They will lay under such conditions as would not be suitable to a light variety, and will "put up" with much rougher climate and also treatment than many other breeds. This is in their favour for a colder situation than the south and Brown Eggs. which makes them even more useful. The colour of the egg varies as in the other varieties, but many of the Browns will lay quite a nice rich-coloured egg, and where the strain is right the egg will be of good size

BROWN SUSSEX HEN.

too. I hope we shall not see the Brown Sussex entered in laying competitions. We must never try to make an egg machine of this fine bird. We have to-day got size and type, and let us be content with doing all we can to improve its table qualities (if that is possible) and not to make a "layer" of it, for if we do this we shall soon sacrifice some of the main properties of the bird.

CHAPTER XVIII.

A CHAPTER FOR THOSE WHO ANTICIPATE.

A Special "Line" to the Beginner.

What breed of poultry shall I keep ? That is often the cry when a person thinks of starting to keep a few birds. To-day there are so many varieties and sub-varieties that it makes it a difficult question which kind to go for. If at all doubtful, try "Sussex." Here you will have the nearest to an all-round, ideal fowl, one which will lay a good number of eggs, winter and summer, one which will act as an Incubator and a Foster-mother, and, further, one which will throw some of the best table chickens which can be produced. What more can one desire from poultry ? The eggs, too, are of nice colour and of good size. If you go for a light non-sitting breed, you get a "real egg" machine, but then you miss the table points in such a variety, and it happens in many cases that "table" is one of the most important.

What Variety.

On having decided to take up the "Sussex," the next question arises : Which variety shall I go for ? There are four ; which one will suit my purpose best ? We will be wanting winter eggs, and we will be wanting

The Lights.

some early spring chicken.   The Lights would be the most useful for the dual purpose, and being hardy and able to stand any soil or situation, they are suitable

Do they Require Open Range.

for all parts or places. The question arises over space required in some cases, and people who have never before bred the Sussex, ask if they must have an open or free range. I have bred and kept them under many different conditions, and can say that they will adapt themselves so well and under almost any kind of conditions that space is not so much to worry over. Of course, a large mob of Light Sussex look at their best when running on a field, and one is not able to breed and rear many chicken in a small confined run. I do not advise such a method, but given a fair amount of room the Light Sussex can be bred and reared much easier than any other medium or heavy breed I know. Assuming that one has a large field at disposal or several acres, and wishes to keep more than one variety, I would, for guidance, put the four varieties in the following order :—

The Value of the Four Varieties.

Lights for eggs and table.

(| |) Reds, in preference to Rhode Island Reds.

Speckled for usefulness and beauty.

Browns for table.

In starting out to keep the Sussex, or, as a matter of fact, any other variety of poultry, one should be certain in their mind upon the following :—Is it to be exhibition or utility ? If the former, then the best bird only should be bought—best for type, feather, size, etc., and these must be managed extra well and taken good care of. If for utility, then buy from a reliable Sussex breeder something which is known to be of good, sound type, and of a proper strain. Do not try to get the two into one. Here is where many people "come down." They send to a breeder and ask for an Exhibition Sussex at utility price. They generally say they do not want an expensive bird, but one good enough to show, etc., etc. In fact, there are people who really expect to get a Palace winner at Egg and table price, and such people often get "let down," for they get "culls," which are generally of pretty low standard. No ; make up your mind which section you are going for, and if exhibition is decided, then be prepared to pay for it. If you are successful you will get your money back in a few years by being in the

Exhibition or Utility.

position of asking a good figure for the birds you have
bred from your high-class stock.

How to Start   Which is the best way to start keeping a few
"Sussex?" There are two systems one can work
upon, and that is, pens of birds or sittings of eggs. The
former is the quicker method, but, of course, costs
more; the latter being quite an easy and fairly cheap
way of getting together a flock; but I ought to say here
that one has to be somewhat governed by the season
or time of the year. Autumn, for instance, one would
have to start with a pen, that is if they decided to go
ahead at once. It would be that or wait until the
spring; and it may be gathered from these remarks
there are two seasons of the year as well as two systems
of starting a pen of birds, and this applies to any variety

Spring or
Autumn.   one may wish to keep. If autumn, then, it must be a
pen. Would we have pullets or hens? Pullets will
last longer, but if we intend mating and breeding the
same winter, it is better to have hens, and mate them
with a cockerel. This gives the greatest stamina in

Hens or
Pullets.   the chick, and makes the rearing easier; on the other
hand, the Sussex being a far more hardy bird than
many, it is not impossible to have good results if
breeding from pullets; and it may be carried out if it
so happens to be more convenient for one to purchase
pullets than hens. I could not advise them, for many
breeds of poultry I know. I have tested most of them
and know what to expect. When should we get the

When to Mate pen and when should we mate? October is the month
to make a commencement. Start off in October and
mate in November or December. Why so early?
Here's the point. The Light Sussex are good layers,
and if hatched early will lay in October and November
same year. So, assuming we have an early hatched
pen of pullets, they will be laying in November and
can be mated, so that eggs from them may be put down

in December. This, not to get early pullets so much Early Spring Chicken. as to get table chicken, for it is the early spring chicken which commands the high price on the market, and it is the early spring chick, too, which is wanted on the table and which everyone likes to see. So it is right to get to work early with this class of bird. How long will it take to get a Sussex chicken ready for table ? This I have often had put to me. I can say that, given fairly good and liberal treatment in the way of housing and feeding, fourteen weeks from the time of hatching, a very useful chicken can be turned out at that age, and, of course, some of them will be ready earlier if size is not so much the object. And so with a small pen of pullets or hens and a male bird, a nice mob may be built up during the first season. All the best and most promising pullets to be saved, especially the early ones, and a few of the cockerels if one thinks they will be demand. Now, suppose we have got through the winter and been unable to make a start with poultry, and in the month of January or February, or even later, Sittings of Eggs. we decide to try a few birds, and as we have to study the cost and outlay, and cannot see our way to purchase a pen of birds, the next best thing is eggs. How to set about it ? We look at the advertisements in the press and are bewildered with the number of advertisements. Everyone having the best stock. I know it is not an easy matter to pick out and select the place or name of the breeder, but much help can be given by looking up the list of breeders of the Sussex Poultry Club, and getting into touch with some of these. Information, too, can always be had from the Secretary of the Club. And so one need not be in so much doubt as to where to make the first purchases. If one has The Method of Hatching. incubators and fosters, it will be an easy matter to get started when the sittings are to hand. But if no machines, how is one to get on ? Buy or hire broody hens. This is possible, and every year I do this. A few good broodies are worth any incubator or foster. Place the eggs under the hens in a properly made sitting box, and get a sound coop or coops ready, so that everything is prepared for the young brood when hatched.

CHAPTER XIX.

How to Rear the Chicks.

I have said "hatch early." This is a point I want to emphasize. It is necessary to do this for the reasons stated in the previous chapter, and there is just one other point I must mention with reference to hatching by the hen before I take the subject of rearing, and that point, in my opinion, is rather one of importance— it is the way to make up a nest. I am not "faddy," but I *do* know that "detail" tells in the poultry business, as in any other business, and unless a hen has a properly made and comfortable nest when sitting, she will not have the best results. There is a method which I have used for hatching pheasant eggs under ordinary hens, and I may say, if one can hatch pheasants successfully, they can hatch anything with feathers. Have the sitting box in readiness, a well-made box, 15 inches square, inside measurement. If to be used out of doors (which I prefer), have a sloping roof. If in a shed this is of no importance. Place the box or boxes on the ground and dig out a round hole in the centre. Should one be troubled with rats on the place this cannot be done, as the rats would burrow underneath and upset the hen during the hatching. In this case it is well to get some 1-inch mesh netting and tack on to the bottom of the sitting box, but in placing this on keep it rather slack so that it may be made a little hollow in the centre. This will be found helpful when shaping up the nest. If netting is used then a few shovelfuls of fine earth must be placed in at each corner, and so a basin-shaped

Making up the Nest.

nest can be formed. The trouble that many beginners
have in getting good results from their hens is not so
much due to the class of hen they use or her broodiness,
but to the want of a proper shaped nest. No hen will
sit well unless she has a proper place to spend her 21
days of rest, therefore every care should be given to
Hay or fine making up the nest. Some people make up a nest of
Litter.
anything in the way of litter they may have to hand.
This will not do. The best material being soft hay or
good soft litter—not straw—to make the nest after
hollowing out the foundation. A band of hay should
be made up and placed around the top of the shaped
nest, and then a little loose hay should be placed in on
the bottom. If this is pressed down well with the hand
it will form a comfortable and proper nest in which
can be placed 15 eggs at any season of the year without
fear of any of the eggs rolling away from under the hen
and so getting chilled. It is all "humbug" for one to
say, as has often been quoted, that only eight or nine
eggs should be placed under a hen in the winter or
early spring. That may be the case if the nest is not
made on the right lines, and even that number would
not be safe in a nest which is "flat," but if the nest is
made up as I have stated, there need be no fear of loss
or trouble, and providing the eggs are fertile the hen
will hatch them all out.

Management
of Hen while   The hen should be dusted with insect powder
Sitting.
before having the eggs placed under her. There are
several kinds which may be purchased from the chemist
suitable for the purpose, and she should have 24 hours
or so on dummy or china eggs before being entrusted
to the sitting. It is well to sit a hen at night; she will
be more tractable and easy to handle if put down on
dummy eggs at night, and on going in the morning to
take her off to feed she is found quiet, and the eggs warm,
she may be given the sitting and placed back upon them.

Now comes the daily management. This is not a troublesome matter and takes very little time, but it must be regular, and it is just this point that so many people fail and say that hatching by the hen is of no use. A hen is reliable—aye, as reliable as any incubator ever made if she is treated right—but I have noticed that so very few poultry keepers give the hen a good chance, and that is the cause of so many failures. Feed her well, take her off at a regular time every morning, and give her water and let her have a good time off the nest to have a stretch and a little exercise, and she will manage the eggs well.

I do not like the sitting boxes which one sometimes sees on the market made with a wire run, so that the hen can come off the nest when she likes. That kind of sitting box generally spells failure. Take the hen off carefully every day at a regular time. I do not mind whether it is morning or evening, but it must always be at one time each day, or the nest will be fouled. Give her a good feed of maize or wheat, but I prefer the former, as it has more heating value, and will help to keep up the bodily heat of the hen. It is the only time I recommend the use of maize as a food for fowls. It is the cause of much trouble when used without discretion.

Hen to be Taken off the Nest.

CHAPTER XX.

THE HEN IN THE COOP.

The chicks should be out on the twenty-first day,
and with a hen that has been sitting well they will
generally be true to time. If the hen is troublesome,
as occasionally they will be through nervousness, the
chicks can be taken away when hatched and placed
in a basket in a piece of flannel, leaving only two in the
nest, but leave them all if the hen is quiet and let them
dry off under her. Have the coop ready, and on short
grass, in a sheltered position. Near a high hedge is a
good place. Have a sound coop with a moveable floor
board; this is very necessary for early rearing, also
where rats are troublesome. Have the floor board
well covered with litter; this to be renewed every day
if possible, for like brooders the coops require to be
kept clean. If rearing the chicks in a garden where
cats may be about, a board and wire run must be placed
in front of the coop, and this run must be used until the
chicks are large enough to defend themselves. Out in
an open field the run is not necessary, and to use it
only makes extra work. Now comes the point of
management and feeding of the young chicks, and
here you will find that if you are rearing "Sussex"
chicks they will be very little trouble, and their hardiness
and quick growth will be a happy surprise to the beginner. Do not give the young chicks food too early
after hatching, let nature do its work in the form of
using up the yolk. Hundreds of chicks are weakened
and killed every season by over-kindness, and the

Putting the Chicks Out.

A Wire Run.

"Sussex" the Hardiest."

Do not Feed the Chicks too Early.

cramming of food into the little chick as soon as he is hatched will have bad effects. The yolk is taken into the stomach on the nineteenth day of incubation, and is by nature used as food for the youngster until it is strong enough to find seeds or insects for itself. I have found out much of the harm done by feeding chicks too early from the many post-mortems I have made, and I have studied the habit of the hen which steals her nest and sits away in a wood or in the hedgerow. She manages her eggs and her chicks in her own way, which, like other animals, seem to be by an instinct, and is generally about the right way, too. Well, if the hen has good results in the natural way, why should we not work close to this way when bringing the chicks out into the coop. Let us, then, take notice of what happens to the brood which is hatched away from the farm or the house. The hen hatches out a good batch of chicks in due course. She does not drag them off the nest immediately they are all hatched. She sits close upon them. She will not even leave the nest for food during the last day of hatching, and I have known a hen to go three days at the latter part of hatching without any food. Here nature is playing a part again. The hen seems to appreciate the value of moisture to the hatching chicks, and she will not get up off the nest because by instinct she knows the moisture will be lost and so injure and weaken the hatch. To all and every poultry keeper I would say, take a note out of the old hen's book here; it is wise. She has a definite purpose, and so she sits "tight" for the first day and perhaps the second day no food, no drink, for the hen does not "suckle" her chicks, although I once had a student who thought so. What, then, does the chick first eat, and when does it first get it ? Remember the youngster is living and growing, and every hour it is getting stronger, every hour it is getting larger, and yet it is eating nothing and only having the *heat* from the hen's body. How, then, does this come about ? Nature—the yolk of the egg. That's it, and that is all it requires for the first few days, and that is all it should have, too.

Seeds and Insects.

In the wild state the first thing the chick eats is small seeds and tiny insects, which the mother hen will find for it by scratching in the leaves and litter. Take note again—Nature. The young chick will immediately begin to hunt for food by scratching in soft leaves or litter, and its food will consist mainly of tiny insects—meat. Here again we are taught something. The chick has already egg yolk, and it adds to the *"meat"* in the form of insects and *"meal"* in the form of *"seeds,"* and here you have the whole art of feeding young chicks, and yet how many people ever give a thought to Nature and its laws. Wrong, my dear readers, wrong ! Everyone of us who bring up live stock, whether it be birds, rabbits or large stock, should make a very strong point of working to the laws of Nature, and by so doing we should not get far off the beaten track.

Day old Chicks.

I have gathered much in the knowledge of running a batch of young chicken by the fact that some people have told me sad tales of not being able to rear chicks which they hatch out on their own farms without heavy losses, often saying the chicks are quite strong and broody when hatched, but soon weaken and die off, only a few being left, and yet—here to them is the remarkable thing—if they send away to, say, a distance of 300 miles for a couple of dozen day-old chicks, it matters not how cold the weather, how long (within reason) the chicks are travelling, but on getting them along and placing in coop or brooder, every chick will grow amazing well and not one will be lost. Yes, I have had scores of such cases in my experience, and there is only one answer to it generally : the birds which are two or three days on the rail travelling are living on the food supplied by nature (the yolk of the egg); the other poor little devils are being crammed with some kind of (mostly unsuitable) food before the natural stuff has been used up, hence the trouble to rear, bowel trouble set up by "acts of over kindness." I could often give that report in my P.M.s, if people would only get the meaning of it.

CHAPTER XXI.

FEEDING THE HEN AND THE CHICKS.

The hen does not require much food during her time with the chicks, and if there is a possible chance of letting her out of the coop with the chicks after the first week, I like to do so ; she will get all her own food and find much for the little chicks. If, however, there should be a number of coops and broods it is not possible to let her have liberty, and so all the feeding must be done in the usual way. A small handful of large grain to be given the hen once or twice per day, that is sufficient.

Mixing the First Foods.

Now, as to the young chicks, there are many different ways of starting chicks, some swear by dry feed, some swear at it, but much depends upon the time one has at

Dry Feed.

disposal to look after the chicks. If they can only pay two visits a day to the broods it seems then only possible to bring them up on dry chick feed, and this can certainly be done, but I do not like it, and the chicks should have more attention if wanted to grow quickly and strong.

Soft Food.

If a chick is wanted for "table," there is no better method of feeding from a start than sifted ground oats mixed with skimmed or separated milk, with a

An Ideal Food for Rearing.

little meat meal added and some rice boiled gently in milk and dried off with the ground oats. Add to this some chopped savoy cabbage and you have an ideal chick food, which I very well know is as near to the right line of feeding as one need get.

I have mentioned "sifted" ground oats, and I think it only right to deal with that subject right here.

It is one of those little things in the rearing of chicks A Strong Point in Rearing. which most people would fail to notice. I have never before seen it mentioned, and I believe is little known, that many chicks are lost—I might say killed—every season by having food stuffed into them which is too "husky," and the young birds are unable to pass the husk, and in due course starve to death with their little crops full and sticking out like a cricket ball. How often, readers, have you opened up a coop or a brooder in the morning and seen chicks come out looking as if they have been fed (by the distending crop), yet the little chaps appear weakly and will totter about quite helplessly. If you pick them up you will find food, or what you think to be food, in their crop. It is "fibre or ash," what we call "husk," and the bird is starving to death. Open up the chick and you will find the crop and main "canal" stopped up like a drain. This trouble I have found by "P.M.s," and I may say that many hundreds of cases of this description have been through my hands, and I feel glad to be able to give poultry keepers warning of it here in this chapter, for it is by no means uncommon, even to the experienced hand, and every year we lose thousands of chicks in this way. It need not happen; just a fine Prevention. meshed sieve, very small mesh, and rub the ground oats through or any other meal of such nature as you may be using. You will often be astounded at the quantity of "husk" or fibre which will be sifted out, and you will soon understand why some of the young chicks have "gone under" when this husky stuff has been mixed in all, or at least the greater part, of their feeds. No, I have often made the remark that before buying food to mix for the new hatch—in fact, long before the hatch is due—one should go to the ironmongers and buy Safe after 6 Weeks. a fine meshed sieve, and make a point of using it always for sifting the meal until the chicks are *six weeks old*.

They are safe after this, as their power of mastication is stronger. Here, then, is the reason that some people "swear by" dry chick food. They say they never lose a chick when using dry feed, but if they give soft food they lose a lot of youngsters. In many cases which I have investigated, it has been found to be due to the above cause, and of course the bad and ill effects of the husky food has passed unnoticed by the poultry keeper until the birds have died. If more people knew the value of a grinding machine for young chicks it would save

Grit. much trouble and disappointment. They should *always* have fine flint grit before them, and if, instead of cramming the young chick with food the first days of its appearance from the shell, it was given *grit only*, there would be less cries of "dead chicks." Fine flint grit should be put down in boxes or vessels in every foster-mother and in front of every coop. It will help even to aid the digestion of the yolk. It is a necessity, and by watching the habits of all birds it can be noticed they want this form of food. No, I cannot call it *food*, but the form of material to assist in *cutting* up their food. All wild birds take it in quantity. Do not mix it in the food, but give it in the way I have stated and the youngsters can take it as they need.

Water for Chicks. Well, I don't care to use water. I prefer milk if anything in the form of liquid is given, but of course few people have this facility. Milk is too expensive to buy for rearing chicken, but sometimes one on a farm has the chance to make use of the skimmed milk or separated, and it should be given to the chicks when possible, far better than letting it all go to the pigs. Water is harmful to chicks unless used with care. By this I mean *always before them in clean vessels.* Here's where the trouble comes. Sometimes the vessels are allowed to get empty and dry, and when filled up the birds drink too heavily, and as many of the common

A Speckled Sussex Hen.
Good type.

Brown Sussex Cockerel.
A Winner, 1919.

A STRONG BATCH OF BROWN SUSSEX CHICKENS.

A FINE TYPE OF BROWN SUSSEX HEN.
A Club Show Winner, 1919.

REARING THE "SUSSEX" UNDER IDEAL CONDITIONS.

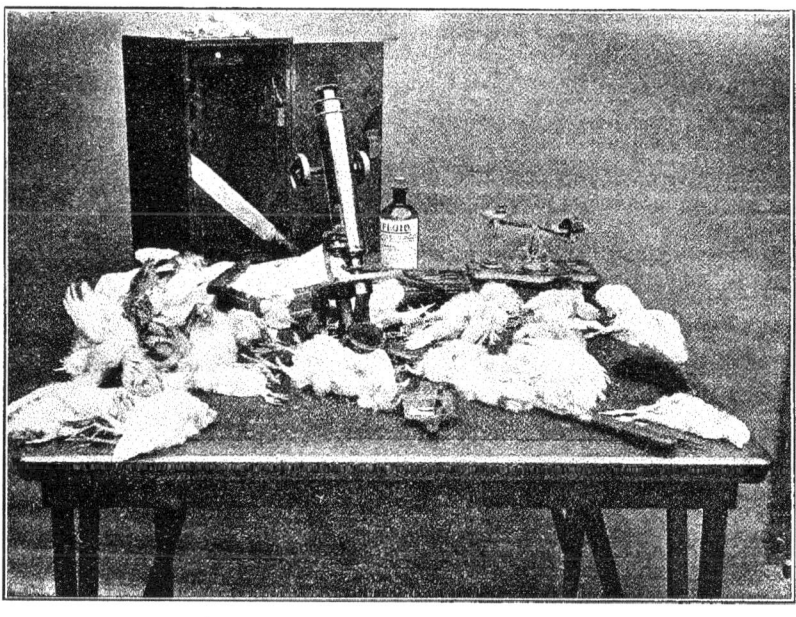

The morning in which I wrote Chap. xxxiii., I received by rail and post, 42 specimens for examination. I put my camera up, and here are some of them.—S.C.S.

ailments of young chicks causes bowel trouble and
inflammation, the action of too much water at one
time is harmful and only goes to increase the trouble.
Keep it always in front of them, if water is to be given
at all, and see that it is in *clean* vessels. Many of the Over - heating Chicks in
coops which are on the market are not made with Coops.
suitable front boards ; they are often made to fit up too
closely in front and admit very little or no air when the
coop is shut up. I often say it would be far better to
leave them open at night and take the chance of vermin,
such as rats and hedgehogs taking the chicken. If a
board is fixed up at the front with only two or three Ventilation at Night in the
holes bored in it for ventilation, it is not enough, and the Coops.
temperature at night under the hen is far too high.
The chicken come out in the morning into a cold,
chilly or drizzling rain, and pneumonia is set up, and the
birds drop off like flies. No, if they have to be shut up
at night see that the front board of the coop has a
9in. by 4in. space filled in with 1in. or $\frac{1}{2}$in. mesh netting,
and this will give them the necessary air.

G

CHAPTER XXII.

WHEN TO TAKE THE HEN AWAY.

There is much diversity of opinion about the matter, or at least there used to be. Perhaps to-day people are beginning to understand more about the subject. There is no need to keep the hens so long with the chicks ; it is a waste of the hen's time, and it is of no help to the growth of the young chicks. They are always found to grow and get away faster when taken away from the hen, so why leave them too long ?   I consider that

When Fledged.

if the feathers of the chicks have become formed, no matter their age, it is time for them to be on their own—some breeds feather earlier and better than others. With the particular breed I am dealing with, the "Sussex," I can say it is a point in their favour that they grow feathers much quicker than most breeds, therefore another point in their favour is that they do not need the hen to brood them for so many weeks. I generally find six to nine weeks sufficient, the longer time of course is the very early months of the year, but they can often be taken away at the six weeks.   The hen will then go on with the egging business, and in due course be coming broody and so ready to take on another batch of eggs and hatch out another fine lot of Sussex.

In the warmer months of the year we find much

Disinfect Coop.

the trouble amongst young chicks, caused by the presence of insect vermin, and much of this can be avoided by the care of the hen, for it is from the hen these

insects are taken generally; there are several kinds of
lice which infest and cause death to young chicks. I
will not go into their life history here, but only say
that if their breathing pores are stopped up the lice will
soon die; they breathe through their sides, and by placing
lard or vaseline on the top of the head of the chick or Dressing for Insect Vermin.
under its wings, both places of which these lice are to
be found, the action of the vaseline or lard seal up the
breathing pores of the lice and so soon destroys them.
No one can rear chicks successfully if they are infested
with insect vermin and will get more of this trouble in
the warmer months of the year. So it will be understood
that the late hatched chicks are more liable to the
common trouble.

The question of what to do with the chicks when What to do with the Chicks when taken from the Hen.
the hen is taken away often puzzles the novice and
sometimes the man who has been at the "game" for
years. It may be due in the latter case to the want of
proper houses, so many young chicks wanting new
quarters at the same time; in the former case it may be
due to want of knowledge as to the birds' requirements.
Do they want artificial heat in any form, etc., etc.?—I
say no. When the chicks have got their first feathers
they can withstand any heat and cold—well, the
Sussex can—they are hardy, and this is where they
are useful chicks for the beginner—no trouble, no
weakness, easy to manage. A "Sussex Ark" is the
best kind of "Cold Brooder" or chicken house I have
ever yet seen. I do not mean the old-fashioned thing
one used to see with a draughty bottom of slats, with
nothing coming down to the floor. I mean the improved Sussex Ark.
kind of Sussex Ark with ample ventilation less the
bottom draught. This is the kind of thing that is useful
to put the young chicks into, when the hen is taken
away. Sometimes one leaves them in the coop, but
generally this is too small, or, at any rate, it *ought* to be,

for with a good brood all reared there would not be room for them, but in the case of half or more of the batch being lost from—shall we say mis-management or bad weather (the latter generally is blamed for losses), then there would be room for the chicks until they were half grown.

Perching. Do not let the chicks perch too early ; that is why I like the Sussex Ark pattern of chicken house ; there are no perches. A bird when quite young has only a soft bone or gristle on its breast, and if allowed to sit up all night on a narrow perch it is likely to get deformed. This is not the only cause of deformed breast-bone in fowls, but it is *one* cause. The main cause is due to inbreeding or close breeding of stock. The feeding of chicken which have been taken from the coops, I will deal with in a further chapter, but I would

Disinfect the Houses. like to mention here that disinfection is absolutely necessary, and every time a batch of chicks are placed into another house it should first be well cleaned down

Place Houses in Shelter. and sprayed with 1 in 40 carbolic acid. Place the houses in a sheltered part of the field and move them to fresh ground frequently ; this is the art of rearing chicks successfully and well and keeping them growing. A meadow sloping to the South and with a stream at the bottom is an ideal place for young growing chicks to run. It is not always possible to find such a situation, but I have been to poultry farms where they could use such ground, but have never given a thought to the value of it for growing stock.

CHAPTER XXIII.

HATCHING SUSSEX CHICKS IN INCUBATORS.

Hatching by artificial means: this is a system which many have to adopt because they have no broody hens, or because they prefer the method to using the old hen. With a breed like the Sussex it is not really necessary, because the Sussex are of a broody nature, and all the varieties make good sitters and mothers, but we must deal with the question, for it sometimes happens one wants get out a number of early chicks and would like to work on the two systems, artificial and natural, so now I will deal with the artificial methods.

There are many different kinds of machines on the market to-day—some better than others—but most of them reliable; it is a question which will suit best, hot air or hot water. I have worked and experimented with most from the first pattern put on years ago by Mr. Chas. Hearson—the now Late, for he has just died— a clever man, who did more for artificial Incubation in the early days than anyone, and he did it by making a study of the old broody hen. In the early years of my first giving lectures on poultry keeping, "The Hearson" was the only machine made in the country that I could safely recommend; to-day there are so many good makes that it would take a long time to make note of them all. The room in which the machine is to be worked is a point worth consideration. We read of Incubators being *run* successfully in a bedroom, in a kitchen, and, in fact, any odd corner of the dwelling house; but this is not giving the machine or eggs quite

Incubator.

Room for the Incubator.

a fair chance, and I always suggest that a separate room be set aside for the purpose, and that this room should be in such a position that the Incubator cannot be disturbed—that is, in a quiet place, just as a hen would be on her stolen nest in a hedgerow. Here we are again touching on the laws of nature: that's it, run an Incubator on the same lines as the old hen sits on her stolen nest and you will be "near the line." I like to work all one *class* of machine in the same room, that is to say, all hot water or all hot air together: we will get the best results in this way. One must use their *Brain* to work a machine with success, and not go too much by books, or by what their friends may tell them.

Ventilation. I am assuming all the time that it is "Sussex" chicken which are to be hatched, and as I've previously remarked they are among the hardiest of any of the present day kinds of poultry, and so with this view in the mind, a few little mistakes will not cause a complete disaster; at the same time, when running eggs in a machine things must be *about* right. The room, for instance, or the place where the machine is being worked, must be well ventilated; fresh air is one of the things which must always be kept in mind. The embryo-chick must take in oxygen through the pores of the shell, and unless this oxygen be pure the embryo will become weak. This means a weakly chick when hatched (if hatched at all); the ventilation must be at the top of the room, well above the machines, not a bottom draught: this is fatal, and is the cause of much disappointment to those who first take up this work. A door opposite an old fireplace and an Incubator placed between will often cause much trouble and bad hatches, the draught going underneath the machine upsetting all **Temperature of Room.** calculations. The temperature of the room, too, is a point to consider; unless a fairly even temperature in the room can be kept up, the success of the hatch cannot be guaranteed—so very much depends upon this—and where one is running more than one machine in a room they can keep a better and more regular temperature— 60 degrees is what I like to see, and with this one can run the drawer thermometer at 104 degrees in most makes of machines with success; if the room temperature falls to 40 degrees or below, the drawer thermometer should register 105 to 106 degrees. The room temperature may be "righted" if one cares to use a paraffin stove; this, if kept quite clean, will keep the room warm and give off no bad smell.

"Sussex" eggs being laid by such hardy fowls Management of Eggs. will stand "travel" better than some, and they may be kept several days before being put into the incubator if one wishes to do so, or is not quite ready for them, but the fresher the egg is used generally the earlier will it hatch, which means that there is more vitality in the fresh egg. As soon as the egg is laid evaporation begins to take place, and so the longer an egg is kept the less "meat" there is in it. Fill up the egg drawers Fill the Drawer. when the machine is found to be running steadily, and shut it up, not cooling or turning the first day; but on the second morning eggs may be turned and cooled for a few moments. Here is another point taken from Cooling the Eggs. nature. I have watched the hen which has stolen her nest and is sitting away; she comes off the nest generally about a regular time each day, and she will be off a considerable time—30 to 50 minutes—until the day when the eggs begin to chip. Then she sits tight, and nothing will tempt her to leave the eggs. A good lesson is learned by watching the old hen at her job in a natural way. It means that we should give our Incubator eggs plenty of time to cool every morning, and it also tells us pretty plainly that it is unwise to open the egg drawer when the chicks are hatching. It is not that

Loss of
Moisture.

the eggs get cold, but it is the loss of moisture which seems to be needed to assist the young chicks in breaking their way out of the shell. These are points which should be considered.

CHAPTER XXIV.

REARING "SUSSEX" CHICKS IN BROODERS.

There are many ways of rearing our chicken when we have hatched them, and much depends upon the season of year whether we use much or little heat. But I *do* know this. There are far more chicks lost every season by *over* rather than *under*-heating. We have to-day in this country large brooder houses with thousands of chicks capacity. I will not deal with these here, but rather to give help to those who only intend or have room to rear one or two small batches. First A Foster Mother. see that the foster is clean, that it has been thoroughly disinfected with carbolic acid or something of such powerful nature. Next bed down well with "cavings" or rough litter. Then see the lamp is clean and the wick dry and new. There are some machines which work only with a lamp and some with a lamp which heats water in a tank. One is as good as the other. But what I do find very imperfect in many fosters to-day Ventilation. is the want of ventilation. When a good batch of chicks are placed into some makes of fosters, the place gets stuffy at once, and should one be trying to work such a machine, air holes should be bored at once. Much trouble is caused by running too many chicks in Avoid Over-Crowding. one foster. People seem to forget that every day the chicks grow, and consequently their bodily heat is greater and they want more space and less artificial heat. What is large enough for 80 chicks at two days' old would surely not be large enough when those birds are three weeks, or even nine days, and here is the

cause of much bad feathering in foster-reared chicks—
overheating and overcrowding. Yes; they are two
of the worst evils in rearing chickens artificially. Just

Clean out Often. another point. When rearing chickens in fosters, they
should have clean litter every other day. Many people
fail to keep the fosters clean and cause all sorts of
trouble amongst the birds ; also it checks the growth,
and this must always be avoided. A common mistake
is to keep the chicks in the heated chamber three or
four days after putting them out ; this is a great mistake
and accounts for great mortality every season. Just

Get them out into the Air the first day they may be kept rather close, but on the
second day and every day after they should be made
to come out into the open. Never mind what the
weather may be, for some kind of shelter can be rigged up ;
the main idea is to make the chicks hardy and strong,
and unless they are brought out into the air from the
first they will become weakly, just in the same way as
overheated greenhouse plants, and they will then look
miserable things which no one can rear quickly or well.

Move Foster to Fresh Ground. We should always remember that when a large mob of
chicks are placed in a foster, the ground around the
foster is likely to get stale quickly, and it is well to
give the foster a "change" pretty frequently. Also

Cold Brooder. keep it in the shelter. The cold brooder should be a
larger kind of structure than the foster, and I notice
that many which are on the market to-day have not
sufficient air space ; they are too *low*, thus not allowing
the hot air to escape. All cold brooders should be well
ventilated and be high pitched, for usually a large

The Improved Sussex Ark. number of chicks are being run together. The improved "Sussex Ark" is one of the best brooders I
have ever seen, it giving space, ventilation, and an easy
matter to keep clean.

Weeding Out. The time soon arrives when the separation of sexes
must take place, although the "Sussex" are not so

precocious as the lighter breeds, and will be all right
up to the age of 12 to 14 weeks ; after that it is better
to have them in separate flocks, and, as I have remarked
in a previous chapter, it is difficult to know if the colour
is coming right until the birds are much older.   Assuming
one is "out" to breed "Sussex" with a view to exhibition, they should make a special point at this stage
to go through the flocks, and any very likely looking
specimens can be improved by taking out and having
extra attention and care ; the plumage can be kept
in good condition if the bird is handled right, and it is
at this young stage when much can be done to ensure
a good colour.   I am afraid too many exhibitors miss Keep the best
this point, some for the want of knowing and others Sun and Rain.
because it entails too much work.   Rough shelters
against the houses where the young birds are kept will
help considerably to keep the plumage good.   Rain is
bad and should be avoided as much as direct sunshine.
Always do the best to keep the youngsters growing.
A check in the early or chick stage will ruin a bird for
either stock or exhibition.

CHAPTER XXV.

SELECTION.

How to select a pen of birds for mating. That puzzles a good many. They do not know what points to go for. Now, if one will turn to the coloured plates in the book and go through the shape, the type and colouring, it will be a guide in mating up. I do not expect everyone to have perfect type and colour as shown here, but that is where the art of selection and mating comes in, to be able to supply the deficiency in the one or the other, and to do this is the art of

Long Back. mating. Take, for instance, the shape of a bird. The long back, which we want to get in all the "Sussex," and which sometimes fails in the hens. Should we have a pen of hens that do not quite fulfil the conditions as to type of "long back," then we should not have to "scrap" that pen of hens, but to try and make up this deficiency by introducing a male bird with that feature extra well defined—a bird which may perhaps fail a little in neck, hackle and other colour, but be extra long in the back and would breed chicken from these hens which would be pretty good to type. The proverbial phrase of the breeder—"Like begets like"—is true. Take the family likeness of children to the parents; it is generally very pronounced, it can be clearly traced and does not rest with one feature only, and another point to note in this, how often we see traits and character in a family relating to the *grandparent*—even to generations back—and so in breeding poultry, whether it be for an egg strain or colour and type, by using brain and common sense in selection the desired results can be obtained, and it is just here where so many breeders fail. They mate *anything* with a pen, trusting to what they call "good luck." This often leads to nondescripts being bred, and then such people will say that there is nothing in the mating; it is not possible to breed more than one or two good birds from a pen. I say that such indiscriminate mating only occasionally breeds (by accident) one or two specimens up to type, and is no credit to the breeder.

Many facts go to prove that every feature in every animal has *some* tendency to repeat itself, and this is found to be the case in the breeding of all live stock, and the aim of the breeder must be to get *all* the tendencies required thrown into the stock which is mated. That's a stong point in mating and one which should be predominant in the mind. To try and throw ALL the tendencies into *one* direction. The question of "yellowness" in the Light Sussex cockerels I have mentioned in a previous chapter, but I want to bring up the question again, because, in my opinion, it is a sad defect in a bird and one that all breeders should do their level best to stamp out. I know too well that it is difficult to handle ; that we are up against something "heavy" in trying to rid it, but it must be done, and I think in time *will* be accomplished. To-day it is almost impossible to find a white-backed Light Sussex cockerel, and at all shows one sees birds with the tinge, and in some cases far more than a tinge. I believe that if we are to breed out the bad colour (and it will only be effectively done by *breeding*, although as I have before said, much can be done by keeping the birds free from *rain* and *sun*), we must make a careful study of the mating, and I have found that the lighter hackled males mated with pure-white backed hens which have good hackles throw males with less tendency to

Breeding out the Yellow Colour in the Lights.

the yellow tinge, but it is only by using this colour of male two or three seasons that we can expect to get the majority of cockerels with a cleaner top colour, and if we go too far we lose in the hackle.

The White Leg.

Take again those unsightly red legs. They are said to be due to the bird having too much exercise. All bosh! It is a trait bred in the bird, and it must be "knocked" out. I want to see *all* of our good Sussex shown with white legs—I mean *pure* white—and it will come, too, if we are more careful in the breeding or mating of the stock. The grand art of mating is not to mate for one point only, but, as in the case with poultry, to mate with the object of breeding for several points, and this is what makes the work so interesting, so fascinating and yet so intricate. To breed for one point only is quite a simple matter, and if the pen should only fail in *one* point the breeder will have very little difficulty in getting his birds right; but on looking a pen over closely, it generally "pans out" that they are lacking, or weak, on more than one point, and it must always be understood that the faults, as well as the good points, of a bird will be reproduced. And, again, it is difficult to say when the tendency will occur to breed some latent fault of generations back—for I believe these can never be bred out altogether, although only a small percentage of the progeny may show it.

Time required to breed out a Bad Trait.

It takes time to breed out the faults in a pen—and it cannot be done in one season—and I often say that a breeder does wrong to bring in fresh blood to try and *alter* a characteristic or fault in his birds, because, although he may get the particular taint out of his flock more quickly by obtaining fresh blood, yet he may overlook a fault in the bought stock, and so breed in something amongst his already nearly perfect flock which will take him years to put right. To sum up the chapter, let me say that if breeders of the Sussex were to mate smaller pens, in many cases they would Mate a Small Pen. have better results with regard to special points, such as type, colour, etc. By mating, say, only two hens with a male bird, and selecting these three for certain good qualities, it will be possible to get a fair percentage of typical youngsters, and then, from this generation, to mate again, and so get bred up a larger number to the points required. This system is the right one, and although may, to some, seem a waste of time with a valuable cockerel, will, I know from practical experience, give the best results.

The term used—I don't like it—''Throw Back'' is ''Throw Backs'' given to nondescripts bred from a well mated and carefully selected pen. I ought to mention this, because it sometimes happens that some of our well-known breeders send out a sitting of eggs at a good figure from the best pens. The pens are well mated, and the birds may be winners, and yet, when the customer has hatched the eggs, and the chicks have grown away well, he is very disappointed to find some ''mismarked'' birds amongst them. He may, too, imagine that he has not had quite ''fair play,'' and that the breeder had put him in some second grade eggs ; but let me say here, one must not judge such a case too harshly. It often happens that from the best mated pen one will get ''throw backs,'' and although very annoying, cannot be called an ''unfair'' action of the breeder who sold the sitting.

CHAPTER XXVI.

HISTORY.

I have on my desk an old book of Poultry, the date of which is 1854, and in this book a chapter is given to the "Dorking Fowl, or Sussex Fowl," and to me— and perhaps to breeders—a few points "culled" from this chapter will be of interest. Note, please, this is written years and years before the Sussex Club was formed, and bears out the statement of some few of us who said in 1903 there *was* such a breed of long standing.

The Sussex Introduced by the Romans.

This fowl, "Dorking," so called from a small town in Surrey, where probably the variety was first systematically and extensively reared (being found there in greater purity and perfection) is undoubtedly a breed of *Great Antiquity*, having been noticed and described in the first century of the Christian era both by Columella and Pliny, and there seems fair grounds for supposing that these birds were introduced into this country by the Romans, among whom they had attained at that early period some celebrity, and were much esteemed. It has been suggested that Shakespeare was acquainted with the superior quality of these fowls, and that he alludes to them in his Henry IV, when he makes Justice Shallow "of Glo'ster," order a couple of "*short-legged hens*," for his guests' repast. This old story goes on to quote that these fowls were raised at Horsham, Cuckfield, and other places in the Weald of Sussex.

I think the word Cuckfield is wrong, and it means Uckfield, because we have proof of the "Sussex" being bred in that district very many years ago, and in the district of Cuckfield there has not been so much poultry rearing. This interesting book goes on to say that, centuries ago, a writer in the *"Gentleman's Magazine,"* remarking upon the number of "Sussex Fowls" he saw at Dorking (or Dorking Fowls) observes that the fowls (especially capons) were "well-known to the lovers of good eating" as being remarkably fine birds. We then get: "It is not at all improbable that what is termed the "improved" breed of Sussex Fowl has originated from a Dorking cross. Let me here say the good folks of 1854 had a fine "eye," or shall I say "taste," for a well-bred bird, and were not bad judges either.

This chapter goes on to say that we do not admit, **Sub-Varieties.** strictly speaking, of any sub-variety of the true Dorking Fowl, but as a mixed breed has, by numerous crosses during a long series of years, become established almost as a permanent variety; under the same name it may perhaps be advisable to treat it practically as a *"distinct branch"* of the Dorking Fowl, which will comprise all the coloured sub-varieties. We shall thus have The Sussex Fowl or "Improved Dorking:"

GREYS.	BLACK-BREASTED.
Speckled.	Silver.
Spangled.	Golden.
	Japan.
REDS.	CUCKOO-BREASTED.
Speckled or Pied.	
Pencilled.	

I would like here to point out the last named on the right of the margin, the Cuckoo-breasted. I have twice before mentioned this "colour," and from the gleanings of this old book it goes to show there *was* such a sub-variety years and years ago. Shall we ever be able to make a revival of this, which, in my opinion, would be a very useful class of fowl, and much ahead of

H

many of the weakly, useless sub-varieties which we have
"shoved" on to the public to-day. We want a "live"
fowl, something which is "good," not a "china ornament,
and these old Cuckoos would be something of the "right
sort." In this chapter, too, a Capt. Hornby writes
with reference to his experience in breeding the Sussex
fowls, and laments his inability to get chickens true to
the colour of their parents, and states that this year he
had four "Spangled Hens" but got scarcely any spangled
chicken, and of these half were "*Double Combed*"—
though the parents were "*Single Combed.*" That
such should be the case is by no means surprising
when the dashes of true Dorking, Malay game, or
Spanish blood so frequently found mingled with the
Sussex, together with the constant tendency in all
mixed breeds to throw back, are taken into account, and
the only wonder is, that, in the face of the strong presump-
tive evidence of cross-breeding which these facts afford,
the Sussex fowls should be found carrying off prizes at
Exhibitions, side by side with the original and genuine
Dorking race—(Now note, please) "not that we wish to
speak in any way disparagingly of the merits of the
Sussex "*As a Fowl*," for we readily admit that crossbred birds often surpass their original progenitors, but
all we contend for is, that as a "*breed*" or "*variety*"
they ought not to be permitted to be classed or to
enter into competition with that of the true-bred Dorking.
Here I would like to "break" in. This shows what
good work has been done by forming a "Sussex
Poultry Club," for they now have classes of their own—
and well-filled classes at that, too. The writer then
goes on to say. In describing the Sussex fowl we may
observe that it very nearly resembles the Dorking in
shape, but the body is rather longer and more squat,
or duck-shaped. It is also a much larger and heavier
bird, weighing from 7½ to 10½ lbs. if a male, and 7 lbs.

to 9 lbs. if a hen. The head should be small, the comb, if single (which is more generally than otherwise), should be large, deeply serrated or vandyked and of bright red colour, with large pendulous wattles of the same ; bill of a dusky ash colour ; neck longer, more tapering, and not so clumsily carried as that of the Dorking ; breast said to be fuller and of better "fleshed ;" the legs longer than the old breed, and of grey or slaty colour. (Author : Not white as we want to-day.) The number of claws on each foot perfectly indefinite, varying most provokingly in some specimens from four to five, and even occasionally to *six*. Those whose birds have only four claws and to whom marks of true breeding are not objects of interest, contend that the "*absence*" of the supernumerary claw is one of the great characteristic advantages of the Sussex breed, whilst the possessors of five clawed fowls contend warmly that the "*Presence*" of that additional claw proves the purity and genuineness of the stock. We must leave the two parties to reconcile the two positions, merely observing in regard to the second that "*although every Dorking fowl has five claws, it does not at all follow that every five-clawed bird is a Dorking.*" The "Grey Speckled" is now dealt with. (I really do not quite know what is meant here by Grey Speckled, but I will give the matter as quoted in this old work, because it all relates to the history of our present-day "Sussex.") It states :—The general plumage of this sub-variety is a dirty white, indescribably streaked or "speckled," with mixed shades of black-brown, and a sort of dun colour, which are more defined upon the breast and underparts. The hackle and saddle feathers are straw-colour with dark streaks or shadings. The tail usually black, but sometimes broken with white ; the legs dusky yellow shade. The hen has much darker feathering, being prinicpally brown, speckled with white, black and yellow ochre. The Spangled are often bred from the Speckled fowls, but differ considerably from them in plumage. The breast and underparts are mottled black and white, the hackle and saddle feathers (the principal distinction) a yellow tinged white tipped or spangled with black and brown ; back and wings blue black broken with dark brown and white ; the long tail feathers lustrous black, and the shorter feathers

white. This is a showy kind of fowl, the prevailing colours being dark rich red speckled or pied with white and occasional splashes of black, the breast is black and white mottled, slightly streaked with red, the hen of a dark brown or chestnut body speckled with white. The "Pencilled" differ from the Red Pied in the body colours, which are white and black only, and are more regularly and neatly intermixed together, the ruddy tinges on the breast being likewise more apparent. The black-breasted sub-varieties include all the darker coloured Sussex fowls, and being rather handsome and showy fowls are generally admired and reared by poultry fanciers. In all probability they are in many instances the result of the system of crossing between the Dorking and the Spanish fowls introduced many years ago into Sussex.

Well, readers, I have given a "sample" of what this very old book contains on the Sussex of the days gone by, and it will be seen that even then there were "Sussex" and sub-varieties of "Sussex," and also that our old "black-breasted" bird crops up. With this I must leave it, and let the reader figure out the old colours and markings, etc., but *must* just add that to-day we have not in *our* standard any colour of a Sussex described as "yellow ochre," but it runs pretty close to the colour we sometimes get in the Light Sussex Cocks—that yellow colour of which I have written so much about.

CHAPTER XXVII.

"FEEDING SUSSEX CHICKEN."

The rearing of early hatched chicks is work which requires care and attention, also some knowledge as to the treatment of the youngsters. As I have before mentioned, the "Sussex" are far easier to bring up than many breeds and are quite easy to rear during the winter and early spring, when the weather is often changeable and wet. Cold weather is not so bad for Chicks in cold Weather. chicks as wet, windy weather; in fact, we generally find they grow away better when it is frosty and cold, this is somewhat due to the ground keeping more clean and also that insect vermin do not work on the chicks when it is cold.

The feeding of young chicks is of importance if one wants to get quick growth and early development. I do not mean by this that they should be forced at all, but the food must be sound and of the right kind. I am very much in favour of soft food for chicks; it is Soft Food. more easily assimilated, it acts quicker and the birds grow out faster on it; but I know many people do not like to use soft food, thinking it causes bowel trouble. It is not the soft food which causes this common complaint, but it is due to other things, which in many cases means rather bad management. Good, sound, well-mixed fresh soft food will never give the birds bowel trouble, but if the food is mixed in unclean vessels Sour Food. and allowed to stand about for some time, then it will set up all sorts of trouble, and this is, I am afraid, what often happens with poultry keepers, and then they blame the food, and say, "Oh, I can rear better on dry grain." Quite so! Such people will rear better on grain because the grain does not require such careful handling; it will not go stale, and is always fit for use. This, however, does not mean that grain is the best food to give chicks to bring them along quickly, and, after all, that is what we all should aim at—quick growth. This means sturdy healthy chicken. I have tried very many systems of feeding during my life's work amongst poultry, and I still say soft food, 75%, using *some* grain to keep the gizzard of the chick in

Number of Times to Feed Young Chicks. action. If feeding on the two systems—dry and soft— I like to use soft three times and grain once or twice. When the chicks are quite young five feeds a day will be right, but after they get three or four weeks old, four is sufficient, and in the later months three times

Regularity. per day will do quite well. The great secret of strong chicks is to keep the meal times regular. If one makes a strong point of regular feeding, they will never have much trouble to bring the chicks up. They know when to expect the food and they will be out hunting for insect life and busy amongst the leaves, but when the times comes around for a handful of grain or a little soft food, they will up around the coops or brooders and wait for it at the same time every day. I have mentioned that ground oats should be sifted for young chicks, and it is most important. Why? Since I wrote that chapter a few days ago I have had three cases of P.M.'s, showing crop trouble set up by using husky meal. You will say, here is another reason why grain or dry chick food is the best and safest to use. Yes; I know that is another point in its favour, but then I also say : If one knows that too much fibre and ash (husk) is injurious to the young chick, they will guard against it, and it is quite easy to make the meal quite free from it. I like to

use a little boiled rice for young chicks ; it is especially Boiled Rice.
useful in wet, cold weather. The starch is good to
"ward off" bowel trouble—boiled in milk when this is
obtainable. Not into a sloppy mash, but only sufficient
to swell and soften, then dried off with ground oats or
some other meal ; it forms an excellent food, and
chicks will go for it greedily—it seems appetising

Groats. This is the Scotch oat or a heavy oat with Groats.
the husk taken off, and forms a useful food as a separate
grain feed ; small or tail wheat, too, is the right thing
to give. I would mention here that I often get enquiries When may
Grain be
Given.
as to when grain, in the form of wheat, etc., may be
given to young chicks ; at what age may they have
this kind of food. Well, if they have fine flint grit in
front of them from morning to night, grain may be
given from the first, but the grit must always be in
evidence.

If poultry keepers would only use more green food The Value of
Green Food.
for young chicks, I should not get so many sent in for
P.M.'s, and the losses in the country every season would
be far less. Savoy cabbage is the best, and some should
be grown especially for the early broods. Lettuce is
good, but does not come in at the time when required.
Onions, too, are fine, and the Tripoli should be sown
in every garden at the end of July, when they will be
ready to pull in the winter and early spring and form a
most useful "bowel corrective." Chop them fine, and mix
in with the soft food. All green stuff should be chopped
fine ; it can then be mixed more thoroughly and none
will be wasted. We must just consider the question of
"Nature" again. The old hen who, by instinct, knows Animal Food.
what to do generally, will take her " wild brood "
down to the edge of a stream, if there is one within
reach, or she will find a "ditch" with a little stagnant
water running near the hedgerow. Now, what does she
go there for ? It is not the water. No, it is the insects

which breed and multiply very fast, and she knows in her old mind that these lively little plump "bugs" and crawley things are good food—yes, natural food—for her offspring, and so let us take a lesson again from the old hen. If by good chance we have a stream near the rearing ground, place the chicks, the coops, the brooders and the houses down near it, encourage the hens to take their chicks there, and, if rearing with brooders, draw the chicks down near the stream by feeding. They will not need much coaxing after they once know it is there, and so by this, one will be giving the chicken natural food, which, after all, *must* be the best, and at the same time saving, to a great extent, the cost of the food bill—two ends gained by common sense. Failing a stream or ditch, we must revert to artificial "insect food," or animal food in the form of granulated meat. There are several forms of meat and fish meal on the market, and most of it is good. A little can be mixed and given to the young birds every day; they do not require a large quantity, and it should be of good quality and free from salt.

To Assist Feathering. We get trouble some seasons with the poor feathering of chicks; some breeds are especially troublesome in this way. The Lights are not too fast in this business in some windy, cold east wind seasons, and perhaps a hint here may be helpful to breeders. Linseed, that's the thing to help feathering. It may be boiled and a little mixed in the food, or, if one does not care to go to this trouble, it can be used in a dry state—just a handful put into a bowl when mixing up the meal for 25 chicks (say, six weeks old). It will help the formation of feathers, and in other ways, too, be good for the chicks. Let me just mention here that one must always be prepared for little ailments and troubles when rearing chicks, and if they set about it with this in their mind, and watch the chicks closely, there will be less chance of disappointment.

Every youngster has an existence of his own; Remember Every Chick has a Separate Existence. he is a tiny little chap when hatched, and is open to develop all sorts of troubles. It is the way of the world and all that therein is ; we are born to fight troubles. Yes, it is so with us all, and it is said the weaker go to the wall, and in the rearing of chicken, one must always be watchful, must always be on the look out for troubles, and these people will generally find that they have the least with the birds. One of the reasons I am in favour of small flocks is because we can keep our eye upon them and "spot" a bird which show some ailment. One need never have fears of an epidemic amongst the chicks if they are watchful, and many losses could be averted if, when one sees something wrong with *one* chick, an investigation is made and the *cause* of the trouble located. That's it ! Read that little sentence over again, and then sit and think about it. Stop the cause, and you've nearly completed the work. More of this when on diseases. Coming to the age of 8 or 10 weeks the chicks can have a cheaper food ; the groats can be left out, the rice need not be used, and the main feeding, say twice a day, may be ground oats and middlings, and a little meat or animal food mixed with cooked vegetables and grain in the evening, three times a day being sufficient to feed birds of this age.

I have not mentioned the value of biscuit meal for Biscuit Meal. young chicks, but when this can be added to the general mixture it is most useful, it *breaks up* and adds to the digestibility of the food, and one can make a better "mixture" when a little biscuit meal is added. It can be given to chicks from the commencement ; and, in fact, I would say it can be given to birds of any age from the hatching up to the laying pullet. It should be scalded before using, and where milk can be used for the purpose it will add to its value.

CHAPTER XXVIII.

HOUSING THE CHICKEN.

Now, attention should be given to the better housing of the young birds; they are too often thoughtlessly crowded into small low-built badly-constructed huts—I cannot call them houses—and then if the birds stop growing or get colds, we hear the cry that the chicks are not a "hardy" breed and are troublesome to bring

Move to New Quarters.
up. I may as well say right here that the chicken are often not moved from coops or brooders into larger quarters as early as they should be, and lots of people seem afraid they will suffer from cold if taken from the brooder when young, but they will always be found to grow faster and are far healthier when moved to fresh quarters, and it is a system for everyone to try and follow out, moving the chicks to fresh quarters pretty often during the rearing season. Let the houses be sufficiently roomy and ventilated; that, on going to open in the morning, there is no warm smell from it, that it does not seem stuffy—that is the best test of the

House Clean and Fresh.
size of a chicken house that one can have. I have seen houses when opened up in the morning "steaming" with the rank heat from the chicken's bodies, and the smell of the house, well, bad, very bad. No one can expect to have a batch of chicks growing away and "doing" well under such a state of things, and all this can be avoided by having sufficient good class chicken houses and not overcrowding. Again, cleanliness plays a great part in the growth of the birds. A "chicken" house should be cleaned out more often than a poultry

house; the number of birds and their growing condition
makes this necessary. I have said, open the house in
the morning, but I would like here to point out that, where
possible, I should not shut them in at all at night,
so that they can be out and hunting for food the first
thing in the morning. Of course there are very few
places so free from foxes as to allow one to do this,
but it is a saving in labour and food when possible.
There are disinfectants on the market which are very Disinfecting.
good and may be used in the poultry houses, but one
can always be made up cheaply by mixing 1 in 40
carbolic acid—one part carbolic acid to forty parts of
water—and with an ordinary garden sprayer, syringe the
house with a fine spray all through the inside. If this
is done frequently it will act as a preventative to many
of the common troubles we are open to get where
several hundreds of chicken are being reared. Lime-
washing a house occasionally is very good, but the Lime-Wash.
mixture should be properly made and applied whilst
hot. Get a few lumps of fresh lime, put into a pail, add
a handful of soft soap previously dissolved in hot water,
put a half pint of paraffin and quarter pint carbolic
acid and slake down with hot water, make to a con-
sistency of point which can be put on with a brush. I Making Lime-
have used sprayers, making the mixture more thinly, wash.
bur the trouble is to get the stuff to work through a
sprayer. I should say, slake the lime and get it down
fairly thin before adding the soap, etc., and one must
be careful to keep well back from the pail when making
up the mixture.

The age to move chicks from the hen or from Age to Move
brooders in houses is sometimes puzzling to the novice. Chicks.
I say the best guide one can have is the feathering and
general growth of the chicks. Some breeds come along
faster than others, some seasons are better and the
chicks grow faster, so that we cannot go so much by

age as by the general circumstances, and if I say move the chicks to fresh quarters when they are found to be nicely fledged, whether that be at five weeks old or eight, then one will be on the right lines. We generally notice an improvement in the feathering after a batch of chicks have been given a house to sleep in. The question "crops" up as to perching; how soon may a chick be allowed to perch. I like chicks to be put into houses at an early age, but I do not like to see them allowed on a perch. The breast-bone at an early age is very soft and pliable, and when allowed to sit on a perch all night—especially some of the badly made perches, which are no more than sticks—it tends to crooked and deformed breast-bones, and this should be avoided, not encouraged. It is well to get the bird three parts grown before allowing a perch, and if the floor of the house is bedded with litter and kept clean the chicks will be far better off on this, and less risk. Numbers to put into a house must be governed by the size of the house and the age of the chicken, but I should like to say here that the best results are got from small flocks—not more than 50—for many reasons, I like this plan. I know that where we run large brooder houses to rear thousands of pullets, we have to put them in large flocks, but I am not dealing with that side of poultry farming here. I am giving hints to those who want to rear utility or exhibition poultry, and to work them upon the best lines, and I say for many reasons I prefer a small mob. They get a freer range. They can be seen better, and any signs of sickness be noticed more easily than in a large mob, and so here, again, comes the question of houses; and it makes me add that there should always be a surplus of houses, for so much depends upon being able to give the birds room as they grow, and it is something like the plants in the greenhouse, they continually

Perches.

Litter on] Floors.]

Numbers in a House.

Room When Growing.

require moving to fresh and larger pots; if this is omitted they soon stop growth ; just so with the chicks ; and the spare and extra chicken houses should be in hand just as the spare pots for the plants. If a beginner will follow on these lines, he never need have fear or trouble with any of those common complaints which I intend dealing with in a further chapter.

CHAPTER XXIX.

SELECTION OF YOUNG STOCK.

We read something of the selection of pullets for egg production, how the birds should be mated and bred, and how to choose the best and most promising for egg laying, but nothing is ever written about selection of breeds for exhibition or high-class work. Therefore, in this chapter, it is my intention to give a few ''points'' on the selection of young birds with a view of choosing those and saving them for future showing. It is wrong to save back birds for exhibition unless they have most of the necessary good points showing which is required by the standard of perfection. Type and good shape is

Type and Shape.
''something'' to have in one's mind when choosing the young birds. A bird which has grown quickly, too. This is especially useful if it is the intention of the owner to breed from it later on in the second year. A chicken which has grown away fast and has feathered well will be strong and hardy, and will throw that trait in the offspring in due course. In selection one does not

Combs.
usually take much notice of the shape or size of the comb. We see birds at shows with horrid looking combs. They may be excellent birds in most of the points, but the comb ''sprigged'' or fallen over, or far too large. Yet nothing seems to matter. The bird gets a card. I know that the comb is not so important as many other points of a bird, yet I do

The Standard of the Comb.
think the time has come when we should try and get a bird showing a comb true to the standard laid down 6 for it. This says : ''Comb single, medium size, evenly

serrated and erect, and fitting close to the head.''
How many birds to-day do we see in the exhibition
pens with combs showing these points. *Very few*!
And I say we must all give just a little more attention
to the selection of the birds with better combs. A
young bird which shows a long back should be saved, Long Back.
even if his or her colour may not be quite up to the
mark, for we must always keep our eye on this useful
quality. A plump, round, short-backed bird should be
culled out, for this type will never be a ''real Sussex''—
length and breadth is what we must have, and this
must always be kept foremost in the mind when making
selection.

In cockerels more particularly do I like to see them
as youngsters rather long in the legs. I always look Long Legs.
upon a long-legged awkward-looking cockerel in the
''chicken stage'' as a promising bird to select, he will
''come down,'' as the term is used, and show good
frame and type when growth is completed. Again, we
should not save back or select a cockerel or pullet which
in the chicken stage shows too much comb or early develop- Not too
ment. We sometimes get a chick which looks very Precocious.
smart about this time and looks the prettiest bird in the
whole mob, comb grown out, and the bird having a very
shapeable look about him ; such a chicken must not be
selected; he is ''finished,'' and if kept will prove useless
as regards size and type. He or she, as the case may be, is
too precocious, and if it is a pullet she would be coming on
to lay at a very early age, giving only a small egg and
not growing out to any size herself. We cannot find
the colour in youngsters sometimes when selecting, and Colour.
as I have remarked in an earlier chapter, we have to
wait for this: often a blotchy-looking speckled chick
will throw quite a respectable colour later on, and we
must therefore not be too particular on the colour while
the bird is in the chicken stage, for he or she may moult

out (chicken moult) and then show quite a nice marking, and we find this is more particularly so with the speckled variety. Having made our selection, say of the earliest cockerels or pullets, for the summer shows, our next work is to prepare them and get them into the finest possible condition—for condition does tell, and the most successful Breeders keep this in their mind. Again to have a bird in "condition" at the Summer Shows is by no means so easy as in the winter, therefore it taxes the energies of the Breeder to get and to keep this condition. First, let me say the young birds must be in a position free from wet, wind, and sun. This is not always an easy matter to arrange, but will make much difference to the plumage and to the gloss of the feather : it is this "gloss" which we want the bird to show, and it is only by careful "handling" that we can get it. A place which is shaded from the sun, a place where the birds can have exercise on short grass, that is what we want for the young birds.

If we shut them up in the training pen too early, we get an enlargement of the comb and sometimes bring the youngsters into an early or forced moult which of course puts them out of the running for the summer shows. It is far better to have them down on the grass until they have nearly completed their growth, but the pens or place where they are running *must* be sheltered. A little linseed given at the time is very helpful and will improve this sheen of the feather, as will also a little flowers of sulphur given occasionally.

To Bring on for the Show Pen.

Do not Pen up too Early

Linseed.

CHAPTER XXX.

TRAINING FOR THE SHOW PEN.

We must always have a few spare birds if our intention is exhibition. We should be prepared for a bird going sick, or going into moult just as show day comes along, or it may be that in washing a slight mistake is made and the bird comes out a bad colour or it may be by unforeseen accident two cockerels get out of the pens and a fight is soon arranged, no referee being present to call time, and the good old sport is "somewhat overdone," and the result is both birds being put out of action for the next show. None of these things should happen, but they are not uncommon, and so we must always be prepared with a few "understudies." A most promising pullet may be put into the training pen and develop a cold; there must be another nearly up to her standard to take her place in the catalogue.

The room in which birds for show have to be trained should be well lighted; it should be roomy and kept in a perfect state of cleanliness, sawdust on the floor is good, spraying occasionally with disinfectant is right, a table in the room where the birds can be taken out of the pens and placed upon, and be made to stand still and touched up with the judging stick; a soft cloth should be rubbed over them—they soon get used to a little gentle grooming and its good for the feathers if done gently. *The Training Room.*

The aim must be to get the birds quiet and tame and used to being looked at, used to being moved about *Handle the Birds Often.*

by a judging stick. All this takes time and patience. We often hear a breeder say he only picked the bird out the run the day before the Show. Well, he is not giving himself or the bird a chance, even if the bird has been previously trained. They should have a certain time to get into the ways of the show pen. A bird that has been handled and properly trained will show itself to advantage. A bird that has not had this training will generally go into the corner of its pen and crouch down or spring about over the pen so that the judge cannot get a proper view of it ; and although it may have some excellent points, these will be missed and the chances of a card are lost. I am writing this for the benefit of men who have taken up the breed and are hoping to do some ''good'' in the show pen. Old fanciers know well the work there is to prepare birds for exhibition, and even they do not always put in so much time to it as they should. It would help the stewards, it would help the judges, if birds which are sent to shows were brought into better form at

Time Required for Training. home. There is no hard and fast rule as to the time required to train a bird. Some will be quite settled down in a week, others may take three weeks. I prefer to pick them up and give them a few days' training in the exhibition room and run them down again for a few days. They are less liable to throw too much comb when treated in this way. A week for a bird which has had previous training is enough. Much depends upon how the birds have been treated during the rearing season. Some breeders handle and train the birds from their chicken stage, and like colts handled young they make the easiest to finish off, and I would advise every man who intends to take up showing to

Wash Legs and Feet. adopt this course. The legs and feet of the bird should be washed on picking up for the training pen. Use hot water and plenty of soap ; also have a nail brush so that the wash may be thorough. When dry a little vaseline should be rubbed on, rub it well into the pores, and use only a little, then with a soft rag rub the legs Vaseline on the Legs and Comb. well so that there is none left on the scales. This will improve and also give the legs a better appearance. The comb should also be treated in the same way, and, if necessary, the head and comb should be washed when the bird is put up, using a soft tooth brush for the purpose. I prefer large wooden pens for training; it gives more room to handle birds which are wild and frightened. The usual kind of wire show pen is quite good enough for a quiet half-trained bird, but a little more room is advantageous when training.

The litter used in the pen should be dry and clean. The Pen to be Clean. I like "cavings" for the purpose. It is short and easily removed. "Cavings" is a term used for the short straw which comes from the screens of the threshing machine, and there is nothing better to be had as a litter for poultry. A little flint grit or road dust may be put in the bottom of the pen before the litter is bedded down. The birds will scratch for it and so keep them in exercise, a point which is often forgotten by some who put their birds up for several weeks.

Always when passing the pens of newly trained birds throw a few grains of corn into them, and then when they get sufficiently tame and quiet to allow of it, open the front of the pen and put the hand in and give them a rub down and gently stroke them.

A bird, like show stock, will look at its best if it Gloss on the Feathers. carries a fair amount of flesh, and a bird in the training pen generally requires a little extra food, or of a better quality than when running; for getting a fine gloss on the feathers there is nothing one can use which is better than thick linseed tea. Boil this and use the liquor and all to mix the soft mash for the birds, and a difference in the sheen of the feathers will be noticed almost immediately. Scalded biscuit meal mixed with ground oats and a little granulated meat, to this add some cooked vegetable matter, and we have a useful meal for the birds in the training pens. A little grit should always be before the birds, and also once a day green food to be given. Needless to say, the pens should be kept quite clean, having a good thickness of litter down and thus to be renewed often. Spray the floor and inside of the training house twice a week with some form of disinfectant.

CHAPTER XXXI.

SHOWS AND SHOWING.

In this chapter I am able to write from two points of view, viz., as an exhibitor and as a secretary of a good many shows. Let me say right here that intending exhibitors should not leave it until the last moment in filling up and sending in their entries for shows. It not only makes the work come very heavy at the office, but it is most unfair to all those who have the clerical work to carry out. There is so much *detail* in running a show that every one connected with it certainly deserves some consideration and help. Yet it is generally the reverse which they get. Surely a fancier knows a few days before the closing date of the show whether he can enter 10 birds or 12, and in what classes. It is the exhibitor who has caused that very unfortunate system which most shows have to adopt, the extension of entries. It's wrong. I've always said so, and have tried to avoid it, but to do so would have meant cancelling the whole show. I may say that at some of the county shows which I have run, on the day of closing entries I have not had in more than 30, and this in a show that finishes up with over 500 exhibits. Let exhibitors keep in mind that they can help the working of a show by making their entries a few days before the advertised closing date. I do not like to see prohibitive prices put against the exhibits in the catalogue, far better to leave the sum out altogether.

Enter Early.

Prices.

Despatching the Birds.

Birds should be sent in time for the penning, but this sometimes is upset by the rail transfer. I have had birds arrive at a show which is to be held on the Wednesday, with a notice saying all birds to be in showyard not later than 9.30 a.m. Wednesday. I have had birds arrive the *previous Saturday*, and at the same show some come in at two o'clock on the Wednesday, and it is not always the railway is at fault. There are some exhibitors who like to keep their birds back to the very last moment, thinking they will appear better in the show pen, but if they think of the work of the stewards who have so many lots to attend to and so many matters in hand at one time, and that at the last moment it will be apparent to anyone that birds which arrive in good time for the penning will have the better chance. I often wish Show Secretaries were breeders and exhibitors. So few are, or they would have more "thought" for the exhibits under their care. Birds which have been on the rail perhaps days are unpacked in due course and put up into the show pen with no food, no water, no greenstuff—nothing. This, I know, is the supposed correct thing before judging, but this often happens the day before the show, and what I am thinking of at the moment is that in very many cases the birds do not get a scrap of green food from the time they leave home until they return. Now, this is not the way to keep birds in show form, nor is it the right way to treat a valuable bird. I say it ought to be compulsory at every show to provide green food for the birds. Ventilation is another worrying point with me. I cannot understand why some secretaries and stewards should be so remiss in the way of ventilation at shows, more especially is this at summer shows, when the birds (and the public) are in greater need of fresh air, and plenty of it, in the show tent or room, and yet

Green Food.

Ventilation in Shows.

one finds the whole place often shut up all around, and
the only fresh air admitted through the door or gang-
way. I consider that stewards who have not had a Handling
Birds at
good deal of previous knowledge at shows in the way Shows.
of penning and unpenning the birds should either be
taught beforehand how to put a bird into a pen or
"leave the work to those who know how to do it." I have
seen much rough treatment in penning during my
experience of running shows, and my own plan is to
call my stewards together before a single bird is penned,
to draft them off to work in "gangs" of three, and so
it is then arranged that with each "gang" there is a
"professional penner." Let every show secretary
make a note of this, and, further, let me say, go beyond
this and see that some such system *"is carried out at
their next show."*

It is a point often neglected at shows, to go around The Pens.
and see the pens are all properly fixed before penning
is commenced; too much is left to chance, the result
being birds getting out during the night, and much
trouble and bother for the one or two unfortunate
Stewards who should be in the show room in the morning. One should be quite certain that all pens are
properly secured; it will save much trouble and annoy-
ance. If there is one thing that makes me "hustle Tidiness in
the Show
around" it is when I see the show room getting untidy. Room.
Yet how often we go to a show and are unable to move
around the ends of the gangways, because empty
hampers have been stacked there. In some cases
they are left out in front of the pens if too large to go
under. At a show recently, I found two trusses of
straw at the end of one gangway, and the people who
wanted to get through that way were obliged to climb
over the straw. I say it costs very little to keep a
show room tidy. Well, it costs more to-day, because
of the high increase of labour payment, but even at

that it certainly adds to the comfort and look of a show room if the place is kept neat and tidy. My plan is to always hire a man for this one purpose only, to go around all day and each day, and clear up bits of paper and straw, and sweep the gangways and so keep the place fit and open and clear for the public to get around and see the exhibits in something approaching

Packing Away the Hampers. comfort. The Secretary of a show should see to the packing away of empty hampers properly. If all the small ones are placed under the staging (not on the top of the show pens, as we sometimes see—ugh ! Unsightly), and a piece of canvas run along to cover them, that will look well and finished. The large hampers should then be neatly stacked away in a spare room or out of the way. When running summer shows in tents, I hire tarpaulins and have every large hamper packed away outside the tent and covered with the waterproofs. In this way all baskets and hampers are easy to find, making the work of the packers so much easier when the time comes for getting the birds away.

I need hardly say that every care must be exercised by the stewards in penning and unpenning the exhibits, to see that the right birds are penned ; also, when it comes to packing up. It is here I have often had the most trouble ; everyone is rather liable to get into a hustle and a few willing, but really unwanted helpers, are frequently fond of setting themselves to work, with a sure view in end of causing trouble. Oh, I've been through it. One does not want to cause unpleasantness, but it is far better to stop such help, and the work gets finished earlier even without the help, because the whole party does not get disorganised, and perhaps held up for several minutes, because a bird is found to

Work in Gangs or Parties. be wrongly packed. If the system is adopted, as when penning the birds, and the stewards work in "gangs," with a reliable "checker," there will be few birds go astray, and so save endless trouble to the Secretary and the Exhibitor in tracing the lost birds in the days following, when it is known that some have gone astray.

The Secretary should always put the first "gang" upon the long distance birds ; let them be the first to be packed, and, further, see that the hampers are despatched immediately to the station, and let there be as little delay as possible, for it is only fair to send them back at the earliest possible moment. The birds have been several days away from home, perhaps, long journeys and a two or three days' show, and so it is only right they should have preference in being returned early.

Pack Long Distance Birds First.

CHAPTER XXXII.

TREATMENT AFTER SHOWING.

When the birds come back, what are we to do ? And here comes in some of the points I have mentioned in the previous chapter. It much depends upon how the birds have been treated at the show to which they have been sent. It may have been a long journey from home ; it may have only been a little trip, but the railway journey has not taken so much out of them as the treatment at the show, if they have been kept without green food, or have been fed all the time upon grain, and the water vessels not kept filled, then they

Toning. will soon show the effects of it, and some "toning" will be necessary. A few drops of chemical food, such as Parrish's, will help the birds, and is good to give any birds which have been to a show or have come off a long railway journey. There is not much fear of a contagious disease being contracted at a show these days, as more care is exercised in this direction than was the case years ago. It is well, however, to examine and see that the birds have not got a cold or any other symptoms of trouble on returning from the show, and should anything be noticed, it will be wise to quarantine them for a few days.

This "after-treatment" applies to all birds which have been travelling, and so let me say that it is very

Feeding after Journey. wrong to feed a bird on grain when unpacking it. A little soft food is the right thing to give, and not too much of this either if the birds have been on the "road" some time. They will naturally be pretty thirsty, and one generally puts water down for them to drink, but if they can spare or purchase a little milk, this will be far better than water for the first few drinks, and will repay the cost. After unpacking the birds they should be put up into the training pens and left for the night, and should the weather be rough, wet or windy, it is far better to keep them in the training pens for a few days longer, but make a point of putting them out as soon as it is safe. We see birds sometimes Do not over-Show which are "over shown." This is cruel, to say the least of it, and, of course, the bird will not last long, nor in the end will it pay the exhibitor, because the bird soon gets run down and will be of no use either in the exhibition pen or the breeding pen. I know of cases which have come under my notice recently of birds having two days' journey, two days' show, and the Secretary asked to pack the bird immediately after the show and send 250 miles to again be penned and stand out another three days in the second show, and then a long rail journey home, with perhaps further bookings in a few days after reaching home. This is too much for the bird, and it does not "pay." It is well to put Grit, a little grit into the bottom of the training pen, for birds which are travelling do not get any of this much needed stuff, nor do they ever get any while at the shows, although I think it should be given where the shows are running more than one day. The grit is more especially wanted because the birds are being fed upon grain all the time, and it is often the want of this grit which will cause a show bird to go sick and off colour a few days after returning from the show. A little linseed should be thrown into the scratching Linseed. litter of the pen; it will give the bird exercise, as much as can be had in a 2ft. pen, and it is excellent for the birds too.

I need hardly say that cockerels which have been taken from a pen amongst others and trained for the show must never be put back into the pen again, or they will fight until ''knocked'' out.

CHAPTER XXXIII.

COMMON AILMENTS IN CHICKEN.

I have frequently said there is too little known of common troubles amongst chicken by the ordinary poultry-keeper. There is nothing one can get to-day which deals with the subject in a practical way. It is useless for one to give the symptoms of a complaint and then to go on to say: "The bird must be isolated and treated with, etc., etc." How can one isolate two or three hundred birds as would often be necessary to follow out these instructions. And how, again, would one be able to treat every hour, or so, as laid down, each individual bird? No, I say, such information is written or given by those who have never reared a number of chicken, and who deal with the subject purely in a theoretical manner, and that is of very little use to the "man in the street." What he wants is to know how to "locate" a disease or complaint, and further, how to "*prevent*" it. That's the word Prevention. the poultry keeper should freeze on to, prevention. Let there be no cause for pneumonia, bowel trouble, jaundice, insect vermin, gapes, etc., etc., oh, and a hundred-and-one little troubles which young chicks are subject to pick up during their first two months on earth, for it is the young chicken I'm out to speak of in this and the following chapters, and the troubles which young chicks get will apply too in a lesser degree to older birds, and the treatment would be about the same in most cases. I suppose there are few people Thousands of Chicks die. in this country have had more chickens and adult fowls pass through their hands for "post mortem" than myself, for over 20 years I do not remember a *week* passing without "p.m.s." At this very moment of writing, I have five specimens on my table outside, and the morning post has just brought in two parcels which look very suspicious. The mid-day post will, no doubt, bring more, and probably this evening another consignment, or eggs "with spots," òr feeding stuffs to examine, and so it goes on. I have given many hours of my life to the study of complaints in chicks, and the study of "p.m.s" has been most helpful; it is most interesting work and I like it. Sometimes the specimens which have been packed up for several days, should the weather be hot, are somewhat "lively" when they reach me, but they have to be in a pretty bad state if I have to pass them by; in fact, I do not give up a "case" unless they actually walk or jump off the table. (I have had cases warm enough for this to happen.)

PNEUMONIA.

I will deal first with the most common complaint which causes much loss among chicks every season.

Pneumonia. Pneumonia, every day during the rearing season, brings me specimens which have "gone over" with this trouble, a whole batch in a brooder will soon be swept off. And because the birds all appear to suffer in the same way most people think the complaint is contagious.

Not Contagious. One naturally would think so, but such is not the case; the reason all the birds show the same symptoms and die in the same way is because they are all kept under the same conditions, which is generally wrong conditions, and I must say right here that it must certainly be a case of "prevention" in this complaint, for there is no *treatment* which I have ever tested and found to cure. With pneumonia it is most important that keen observation be kept on the birds, and if any sign of the trouble for the cause to be removed immediately.

I am writing as if the "cause" *can* be removed, and I
do so because I know *this* in hundreds of cases is so.
The cause of this troublesome complaint is overheating, Cause.
and then a chill. There you have it, and it is one of
the most common causes of losing young chicks in a
brooder. Remove the cause and the birds will soon
recover.

The symptons of Pneumonia can hardly be mis- Symptoms.
taken if one cares to get the following into their mind.
If affects the chicks suddenly, they may come out to
feed in the morning and all appear to look right. Unless
one is very quick of sight they will notice nothing
wrong, but at the next feeding time a few of the chicks
appear listless, and huddled up in the heating chamber
of the brooder or in a corner. The next feeding time
one or two more may be noticed showing similar
symptoms and by the next day these birds are dead
and others have failed. The trouble is most prevalent
in brooder reared chicks, and it will attack them from
the age of a week to eight weeks. Three weeks is often Age of Chicks
the time when the losses begin, and I trace it to over- with Pneumonia.
heating, overcrowding and want of top ventilation in
the brooders, or when it happens among hen-reared
chicks it is traced to want of room in the coop, the
-front board of the coop being made with little or no
ventilation, and so the chicks are being overheated at
night. Now it will be easily seen that all these evils
may be avoided, and if they are seen to, one need have
little fear of the dread disease attacking the birds.
Occasionally just one chick in a batch may develop
the trouble owing to getting a sudden chill when going
outside the brooder. When we get heavy gales and an
east wind blowing we must be prepared to put up
thatched hurdles or some kind of shelter around the
coops or fosters; it will perhaps save losses from this
common complaint. There are other diseases which

chicks get and show very similar symptoms as I have
above described, but if one cares to take up a chick
which is suspected to have Pneumonia and listen
closely by pressing the side of the chick to the ear, it
will be quite possible to *hear* the congested lungs, the
sound being a sharp crackling noise. There is no
mistaking this sign, and it is a very good test. To
avoid losses from Pneumonia move the chicks into larger
quarters before they become overheated. Remember,

if they are growing they are every day gaining in bodily
heat, and more space is required to prevent overheating
and overcrowding at night, and the reason for so many
chicks getting the complaint at the age of three weeks is
due to the fact that at the age they require more room
in the brooders or coops, and not getting it, soon develop
the trouble. Always leave open the "top" of the
brooder by placing a block of wood under or by some
other easy means. Most of our brooders would be
better for more ventilation.

CHAPTER XXXIV.

INTESTINAL WORMS.

I will next deal with a very common chicken trouble and yet so little known by breeders. This is a contagious disease and will spread amongst the whole flock quickly, especially the younger birds. It is contagious by being spread from one to the other through the excrement on the ground and in the houses. The chicks at six weeks old may seem to be going on all right, Symptoms. they feed well, but on looking closely at them they do not seem to be growing as fast as one would like to see, and on taking a chick up in the hand it is found to be rather light. There seems to be some signs of bowel trouble, but we just put it down and think perhaps it was a rather weakly hatched chicken; such however, may not be the case, it may have been a strong chick, but has got hold of that dreaded intestinal worm which is gradually sapping the life away, for it does not act so quickly as some diseases. The birds will be noticed to droop the wings and stand huddled up in a corner, they close their eyes and seem very drowsy. If one calls them and throws down food they will rush out for it and eat it eagerly, and this is where the poultry keeper is deceived. He thinks there is nothing wrong Always Hungry. with the chicks because they eat well, but with this trouble the birds are always hungry, and their appetites keep good to the last. The cause of the trouble spread- Cause. ing I have given, and the cause of its appearance amongst a batch of chicks is due to foul ground, stale land, ground on which a previous lot of chicks have been

reared, a brooder which has been used on the same
little patch of ground for two or three batches. All
this goes to favour this destructive worm, who, when
he gets into the intestines burrows in to the outer walls
and in a short time right into the intestines, and so
perforates it like a piece of zinc. Hence the noticeable
bowel trouble at certain stages of the trouble.

Prevention.　It will be seen that prevention of this very common
trouble is quite simple and within the reach of everyone
who rears chicks, yet one neglects to move the brooders,
and one neglects to make use of a fresh corner of a field
or a little piece of land which is fresh, or they neglect
to spray the brooders or chicken houses, and to clean
out as often as they should : all these little points making
towards the starting of this complaint. See to these
points and there will be very few losses from the intes-
Treatment.　tinal worm. If, however, the trouble breaks out the
treatment is pretty sure and easy, move to fresh ground,
spray all inside of brooders or house with solution of
carbolic or some such preparation as is sold to-day,
clean out and keep clean the houses and coops, etc.
Treat the chicks by giving a few drops of turpentine in
their soft food, give this the first meal in the morning.
About two applications will clear the birds of the worms
and the action of the disinfectant upon the ground and
in the houses will free the land from the trouble. In
the treatment of diseases in poultry, everyone who
intends to treat a bird must first be sure to remove
"the cause of the trouble." It is useless to give a
chick treatment unless the cause is removed, because the
bird will fail again at once, but here is a point most
poultry keepers up to the present time have failed to
follow out.

CHAPTER XXXV.

THE GAPE WORM.

Years ago I remember that "Gapes" in chicken was a recognised form of mortality, so much was that so, that the "Sussex Hen Wife" thought something was very much wrong if she did not lose from 30 to 50 per cent. of her chicks every season from the gapes. No attempt would be made to stop it, and it was accepted as a regular fate; to-day we have remedies which are pretty quick and sure for the treatment of the chick with gapes, and no one need lose three per cent. of their birds from this complaint. Gapes makes its appearance very suddenly on Cause of Gapes. some rearing grounds, and one must keep a sharp look out if the trouble shows itself, because treatment should be given immediately or the birds soon gets into a weak state and when treated may die from exhaustion. Some soils are more addicted to the gape worm than others; a wet or marshy situation will be one likely to give chicks gapes, this being due to the gape worm or embryo hatching out in moisture. Some land will carry gape worm owing to the chickens being crowded upon it and making it stale; and so to prevent, one must Prevention. see the ground's fresh and clean where the chicks are to be reared. If water is given to the chicks it must be in clean vessels and must not be put out into the sun; warm water will cause the embryo gape worm to develop rapidly.

There are several means of treating a bird with Treatment. gapes, and most are effective. Individual treatment may be either by carbolic fumes or a feather with a drop of turpentine; both are quite safe to use if a little care be exercised. The carbolic treatment is used

as follows : A little carbolic acid put into an old spoon, heat a brick on the fire and when hot take out, place on the floor and put the spoon with the carbolic in it on the hot brick. The chicks which are to be treated should be put into a wicker basket, and as soon as the fumes begin to rise from the brick, which will soon happen from the heat, the basket with the chicks may be placed over and quite close down to the brick, keeping an eye on the birds to be ready to take them out before suffocation; they will stand a pretty good dose, and the action of the carbolic fumes will kill the gape worm; the birds will be quite well and strong by the next day.

The method of treating a single chick with a feather may be useful where only a very small number of chicks are kept, or when only about one or two become affected with the gape worm. It is a simple matter to get a hen's feather—a good stout and stiff one—strip it down to the point within half an inch, only just leaving a few feathery parts at the tips then get the chicks in one hand, the feather in the other, put a drop of turpentine on the tip of the feather and force it down the windpipe of the chick, turning it around quickly, and in drawing out it will often be found parts of the worm drawn out and sometimes the whole worm alive. This may be repeated twice, when the chick should have a rest of an hour or so, and if necessary can then have another dressing, but if properly handled only one operation is necessary. When treating with the feather one must see that the feather goes right

down into the trachea or windpipe; on opening the chick's mouth a small hole is found at the base of the tongue, this opening and closing as the bird breathes; this is the trachea in which the feather has to be pushed down, and it is not so easy at first to get the feather in place.

I suggest that we practise upon a large and older bird first, and with a little practise the small ones can be handled. There is just another point with reference to the method of treatment, I would like to mention, and if one will go to the trouble of cutting open a young chick which has died from gapes, it will give them a chance to see that most of the worms which are found in pairs sticking to the windpipe of the chick will be located at the *lower* end of the windpipe, and when "beginners" first use the feather treatment they often do very little good, because they are afraid to push the feather down far enough, they only put it down about an inch or so, but it should be run down as far as it will go, and when done quickly will "break up" the bunches of worms and not harm the bird. We next come to the treatment with "powder," such as Camlin or Blackerite, and which can generally be purchased at all corn or poultry food specialists, together with the "bellows" for distributing. It is quite an easy matter to treat several hundreds of chicks in one evening by this method, and it is very effectual too if properly carried out. Two, or at the most, three "doses" are sufficient to stop the worst cases. But the directions are not, in my opinion, "laid down sufficiently strong." There are a few points in connection with the way the powder is used which make all the difference to the results. For one thing I have never found the treatment to be so successful if the powder is not fresh, or if it has been allowed to get a little damp—be careful of this always. Again, I would point out that unless the coops are made pretty airtight when the chicks are being treated, the application will not be so effective. In this method of treatment there is no need to catch up the chicks to place them in any particular room or box, but they can be treated in their own coops or brooders, but this should be done in the evening, and

Put Feather down Deep.

Powder or Camlin Treatment.

on a still evening too, for if it is rough and windy the powder will soon be lost and the operation useless. The way to set about the work is to fill the bellows (there are three sizes and I prefer the largest) with the powder, place some sacks or other covering over the coops or brooders, so making them as nearly airtight as possible, then place the nozzle of the bellows *under* the coop, or if it be a brooder, through a small hole made near the bottom, and give three or four blows with the bellows, puffing the powder all in amongst the chicks. The action of the powder loosens the gape worm and the bird coughs it up. The sacks or covering should be left over the coops or brooders from 10 to 20 minutes, and so keep the fumes in and among the chicks. It will be seen from the above remarks that it "pays" to go into the detail of the thing, and do the operation properly, and if it is carried out as I have advised, there will seldom be necessity for a second "doing." I have treated many thousands of chicken, pheasants, and turkeys in this way, and can safely say that none need be lost with the gapes during a whole rearing

season if taken and treated in time. I ought to say that a little lime put on the bottom of the brooder or on the floor board of the coop will help matters just before the chicks are to be "blown." I have known of cases where the worm has been loosened and coughed out by the chick, and the next morning, before the chick has been let out, it has picked up from the floor some of the expelled worms, which have again got into the windpipe, and the chicks in a day or so are as bad as before. To prevent this kind of thing happening, a little fresh lime should be sprinkled on the floor before treating, and the next morning this should all be swept off clean and burnt. Before leaving the subject, let me say that in all cases of "gapes" it is best to treat in the early stages, not merely because it is easier to cure, but every hour makes the chick more exhausted, and so they should have a quick treatment. There are other methods of treatment, but I have given three, which is enough and all of which are reliable.

CHAPTER XXXVI.

THE CHICK THAT DOES NOT GROW.

We get one in a brood sometimes which seems to keep the same size for weeks and weeks. We find more than one in a brood in some cases. What is the cause of this if one or two are backward and do not develop? It often puzzles the poultry-keeper to account for this trouble. Or, again, take a mob in a fostermother; perhaps half of them are quite well grown and strong, while the remaining half are small, undersized, miserable-looking objects, with nothing right about them except their appetites, which grow greater and greater every day. These—drones, shall I call them—although so unsightly and apparently useless, eat as much food as the other half which are "doing well." What then, can be the matter with them, and what can we do to make them look better and

The Cause. grow faster? The cause is rather baffling to the ordinary poultry keeper, who does not "live" with his birds; and however keen an eye one may keep, they cannot always tell when this stoppage of growth first starts, for it *is* a stoppage of growth, and it takes some moving again, too. I am sometimes inclined to think it would be better if such birds could be counted as dead, for they are the cause of much trouble. One cause for this, then, is due to a "chill." It takes the chick suddenly, and in many cases in the form of pneumonia, which they recover from; they may be noticed to be only ill a few days and then appear to get well, as the appetite is good; but could such birds be marked, it would be found that they would not put on 2 ozs. of weight during the next fortnight. They also are feverish and will always drink a lot of water if they can get it. Another cause is due to want of vitality in the egg or embryo in the early stage before hatching. *Pullet eggs* will throw some of these miserable specimens, but in this case the chick will be noticed to be smaller and more weakly when first hatched. Needless to say, such chicks should not be kept for stock purposes whatever the cause of stoppage of growth may have been due to. Such birds should be marked for killing off when just large enough for the table. I often am asked, is there any treatment for such birds to make them "get a move on?" Yes; they may be "hustled" somewhat by using extra stimulating food. I like to give such birds a little chemical food in their meals, and extra rations of meat meal; also one should take these small chicks from the faster growing ones. Keep them in some nice fresh corner on their own, where they can scratch about among leaves or on a dry bank. If poultry-keepers only knew the value of a little sheltered corner of a field for "hustling up" the growth of backward chicks there would be more use made of such spots. Oh, the mortality I see every day of my life in young chicken caused by the want of using a little common sense! During the last three days of writing this book, I have had 42 chicken sent to me for p.m. Yes; this besides several adult birds, and at many places I am in touch with hundreds are dying every week; and so much of the trouble due to trying to rear the chicks unnaturally. Appliance makers tell the would-be poultry keeper that this brooder or that is the best on the market; that all one has to do is to place 100 eggs in an incubator, turn them twice a day, and in 21 days they will hatch 99 chickens or thereabouts.

Treatment.

A Fresh Scratching Corner.

Then put these chicks out in the brooder and just give
them a little dry chick food and water, and there will
be no trouble whatever.   The chicks will, in fact,
according to these smooth-tongued merchants, rear
themselves, and not even cost money for food.   Why
in the name of goodness so many keen people will get
"had" in this way I sometimes "wonder."   I do
really believe if they were told that by using a certain
kind of brooder all the chicks would come on as pullets
they would believe it.   My word! we've something to
learn about poultry keeping and especially chicken
rearing in this country yet.   But let us get well into the
back of our heads that it's "nature" we must take
our "hints" from, and she will give us lots to work
on if we will only have the sense to ask her.   Let us do
this instead of following out so much of the piffling
humbug which we see in some of the papers to-day.
Let "Nature" be our tutor, and then we shall see the
advantage of making use and following out her ways.
Put you ear to the "cackles" of the old hen who has
stolen a nest and has hatched out the brood under the
hedge; watch her doings at every turn; make mental
notes of them; store them up in your mind, and then,
when the time comes for you to run a brooder, or in
any other way to rear some chicks, put these "hints"
shown to you by nature into practice, and I'll say
to you it'll be astonishment—the sound teaching you
have learned.   Make use of every little sheltered corner
to rear a little mob of chicks ; make use of any place
where dry leaves can be found for the chicks to scratch
in.   I know people who put hard, dry earth in their
fosters for the young chicks as bedding.   How in the
name of goodness can they expect the chicks to work
for their grain ?   A chick wants something light to
scratch in ; something natural like leaves or dry litter ;
something which it can move easily with its feet.

Watch a brood of healthy little "wild" chicks hustling the leaves one way and another working for a few insects or seeds. See how quickly their little feet and legs will work. It is an interesting sight; yes, an instructive one, too, if one will only make a note of it. The birds are hunting for their food; they are hunting for it as their ancestors used to hunt, as the Gallus Bankiva or Jungle Fowl of India used to hunt; it is their own way of getting food. They are not taught how to do it for it comes to them in the natural way, and yet to-day—even to-day, as I am writing, even in these enlightened times—we are trying to make ourselves believe that we can bring up chicks in an entirely opposite way to nature. Ugh! It makes me cross to see the stupidity of some people.

CHAPTER XXXVII.

JAUNDICE.

Few who rear chickens appear to know that they suffer from jaundice, and not only do they suffer from this complaint but many hundreds die off every rearing season through it. I have noticed in my p.m. work that more cases of this kind are recorded in seasons when we get wet and cold weather, and such an April as we have just passed through bears out this statement, for I have had many cases of jaundice to deal with during the past few weeks. So a hint right here may be worth considering by those who rear a number of chicks every year, to keep a very sharp lookout in a wet season for this trouble. Another reason why the most dry part of the field should be used to put the coops and fosters. High and dry, but well sheltered, is the place to rear and keep free from this trouble, for if it once starts in a flock, it will affect most of them, and it is very difficult to get them through without loss. I get the greatest number of cases from foster or brooder-reared chicks, so this points again to "chills," the most common cause of so many of the youngsters' ailments. The age of the chicks most likely to get the trouble is from the 3rd day to the 6th week. After this age I seldom find a case, but I often have cases at the early age, and I know that very many chicks are lost during the first week from this cause. Prevention is the plan to adopt. Keep this well in mind, and act up to it, for there is little chance of saving the bird's life when once it gets an attack of jaundice. How do we prevent it,

(marginal notes:) Cause. / Dry Ground / Brooder Chicks. / Age of Chicks most subject to the Disease. / Prevention.

then? By using the right kind of food in proper quantities, and at the right time. Irregular feeding is conducive to jaundice. Also keep the birds on the "cool side" in the brooder; with chicken in coops being reared by the hen; see that there is ample ventilation when the chicks are shut in at night. These are the preventive methods to be carried out, and if they *are*, one will seldom get an attack of jaundice in the chicks. I have found no cure for the very young chick—it generally dies before anything can be done to relieve it — but the older chick may recover if fed chiefly on dandelion leaves chopped fine and mixed in with bread or biscuit meal which has been scalded with milk. A pinch of Glauber Salts, too, is very good to use, but all the treatment in the world will be of little avail unless the "*cause*" is first removed. We must always keep this idea in the front of our mind—remove the cause, and then our treatment will have effect. But unless we do this, other birds will fail in the same way, and so we shall go on having losses. I need hardly say that the brooders and coops should be kept perfectly clean if the birds have a touch of jaundice. Well, in fact, they must *always* be kept clean, and then there will be less chance of them having any of these ailments. The inside of the brooders and coops must be sprayed with a solution of carbolic, and the outside range must be fresh and sweet.

CHAPTER XXXVIII.

INSECT VERMIN.

There are several kinds of lice and insects which are troublesome to poultry, but as my aim is to deal entirely with chicken ailments, I need only mention one or two which we find more commonly upon young chicken, by some people said to cause very little harm. No one would ever make the old Sussex fattener believe that insect vermin were of any harm to birds. He would say, "all bosh gov'nor, all bosh I say. I never seed a chicken yet wot hadn't got lice, nor nobody else, and I reckon tis good fer em I do."

Yes, they would never trouble about lice upon the chicks, but then they used only to have the birds on their hands about a fortnight or three weeks, when they would be ready for killing for market. Yet in tests I have made with the fattening, cramming and preparing for table, I very well know that the chick which is *clean*, free from insect vermin, is the chick to put on flesh quick and turn out the best when killed. No bird infested with insects can be in a happy state and the insects suck and sap certain juices too which tend to weaken the bird; in fact, I am coming to the point where I have had many cases in my time of whole broods of chickens being killed off by insect vermin only, and the difficult thing many times appears to be able to locate the trouble, hence I will give pretty full detail of the symptoms. I have often met people and seen cases where they have dosed the chicks with castor oil, or given them salts, or some powder in their

Lice will kill off whole Broods.

drinking water, trying of course to save the chicks, to give them appetites, and so here again it is a case of removing the cause. I will give an instance of what often happens—this, too, particularly in the warmer months of the year, for it is then that the insects breed faster and grow very quickly and become very lively, like flies. It is when the weather gets warm a particularly sharp look-out must be kept on the broods under hens, with foster or brooder chicks we do not get so much of this kind of trouble, especially when the brooders are often sprayed out. I have been called in to give an opinion on the cause of death, say of one brood of chicks out of five. There being five coops in a row, with one that the chicks have been failing one after the other until they are nearly all gone. When such symptoms show we can generally put it down to death from insect life. The hen has not been "dusted;" Symptoms. she has had lice (the large flat yellow one) which have got on to the chicks as soon as hatched, and in a week has made them most miserable-looking objects, dying one after the other, chirping about inside and outside the coop all day long; that's the symptoms one sees when a mob of chicks are worried by insects. There is another form of insect, black in colour, which may be found on the head of the chick, and about three of these merchants will cause the death of a chick in a week. I have found these amongst foster-reared chicks too. They cause a lot of trouble, and the chicks will get into a most miserable and dejected state unless relieved of these "tenants." A chick who has two or three of these long black insects upon its head will have a very listless appearance, feathers ruffled, closed eyes, standing near the coop or brooder for a long time in one position, and then suddenly seeming to wake up and give a dash off at a great rate, as if to get away from the irritation, which no doubt is really the cause

for the sudden movement.   One can generally diagnose
a case of this kind if they care to take the trouble to
watch the birds, and again let me say that the man
or woman who keeps an ''eye'' upon the chicks, note
their movements and ways every time they go around
to feed, will always be able to locate trouble in time
to treat them and so save losses.   I know a good many
people who, not wanting disease and trouble amongst
the chicks, will never think of looking for it, rather
they blind themselves to the fact that there cannot
be anything wrong with the birds.   Such people will
always lay themselves open to the greatest number
of complaints and ailments, and will not be able to deal
with the cases, because they are let go too far before
being taken in hand for treatment.   The person who
is out to rear a number of chicks and rear them easily
must always be on the watch, on the look-out for trouble.

reatment.   It is not a difficult matter to get rid of insects upon
chicks, but it takes time and patience.   Perhaps the
first application will not kill all the lice, and even so
it will not kill the ''eggs,'' which in due course hatch
and grow and soon become troublesome, and here is
the cause of poultry keepers having continual trouble
with insect vermin all through the season.   They say
they have dressed the hen or the chicks two or three

'll the   times.   Yes ; but they have not done it at the *right*
mbryo Louse. times ; they forget about the ova.   They should treat
the dressing of hens or chicks for insect vermin in just
the same way as one treats a rose tree.   If we make up
a good ''wash'' for our trees and syringe them well,
we find in two days the lice have turned brown in
colour, or, in other words, have died ; but if we look
very closely on the third or fourth day we find a number
of small lice which have hatched out and come to life
since we dressed the tree.   Here, then, we have a
guide in dressing poultry.   Wait two or three days and

then give another dressing. This will kill the second crop or newly hatched lice, and in this way the birds are got clean. Any good insect powder will answer the purpose, shaken well into the feathers, especially Grease or Vaseline under wing and tail feathers. Lard or vaseline will kill the lice which worry young chicks ; just rub a little on the top of the head and under the wings of the chick. Where a brood has been affected with insect vermin the coop should be fumigated before another Fumigating brood is put in. To do this cover the coop well with sacks and get a little sulphur, set it alight on a shovel, or place it on a brick and put it inside the coop, cover up and let it burn out. Do this in a shed or in a sheltered place. This will be useful to remember if any contagious disease should ever break out and the houses and brooders have to be fumigated. After doing this it will make a finish to the work if the coop is sprayed well inside and out with the carbolic solution. There will then be no fear of any infection from the coop, and may be the means of saving much loss and disappointment.

CHAPTER   XXXIX.

CATARRH   OR   SQUACKS.

One of the most troublesome and, I think I may say, the most common ailment in chickens during the summer and autumn months.   At one time I remember one could not go to many chicken rearing farms in the South of England where the trouble was not in evidence, and although in some cases the actual deaths in the flock from this cause were small, yet the loss in the growth and consequently the market prices of the bird was heavy.   I know that some poultry keepers, more especially those who used to rear crossbred chicken exclusively for the table, used to take it as an evil spirit which *must* make its appearance every year, and, of course, it would get worse each year if nothing was done to try and prevent or stop, because the land would be getting more sour each year.   I have been into fattening sheds in Sussex and seen 5,000 chicken affected with catarrh, or what the fattener calls "squacks."   As I have previously mentioned, the term somewhat denotes the sound.   It is a most dread

A Dread
Complaint.
disease, and one which takes a lot of clearing, one of the most troublesome to handle, highly contagious, and here we must stop and ponder.   Just read that line over again—troublesome to handle and highly

Highly
Contagious.
contagious.   I know what I'm writing about.   I've had much to do with this dreadful ailment in my years' working amongst some of the largest chicken rearing farms in the country.   When we get, or are tackling, a disease which is infectious, we have not only got to use care when really handling the chickens which are

ill, but we have to be most careful in and on the whole of the establishment—the houses, the water vessels, our own clothes, boots, hands. Yes; this is where so many fail to "cut out" a contagious ailment. They kill the germs and cure a few birds in one field, one part of the farm or in one house, and they carry on their own boots or clothing the disease germs into two other houses or to other parts of the farm, and so it goes on. Kill and cure, and on the same day set up two more fresh cases. I have seen this sort of thing go on many times. Contagion can only be dealt with Disinfect. in one way, and that is by continual disinfecting; the continual use of a high grade disinfectant, and this must be done thoroughly, or it may as well be left alone and let the birds live, die, get better or whatever may happen. And that is why I call this such a dreadful ailment, not because we lose so many birds from it as in some other contagious diseases, but because of its troublesome nature, the difficulty of stamping it out, the loss of growth in the birds, and the fear of something even worse coming after. That sums up what I think about catarrh. The causes are not far Causes. to seek. Sour land is, of course, an incentive, but the first cases are generally set up by "*overcrowding in small stuffy sleeping houses*"—there you have it— insufficient air space at night. The birds get over-heated. It is between the ages of 10 to 20 weeks, Age. when they are most liable to the trouble. If, however, it gets a hold upon the place the whole mob may get it, from quite young chicks up to the stock birds, and it will not stop at catarrh then. It, therefore, goes to show "that we should tackle" the trouble at once and use all the means in our power if we see the least sign of its appearance among the flock. The longer it is left the greater will be the task of clearing it from the birds.

There are more ways than one of treating or stamping out, but in all it means "work"—it means "sticking to the job"—and unless one can do this it is going to be a heart-breaking business, for as fast as one house or pen is cleared, another starts away with it.   I want to make it quite plain that the symptons of catarrh are somewhat like (in young chicks) those of gapes in its first stages, and is often mistaken for that complaint by poultry-keepers—understand, it is only in the first stages that this is so—and to one who has had dealings with the trouble before they will never mistake it; but I am anxious to make this quite clear to the—shall we say ?—novice, because the disease is one which requires immediate and careful treatment quite different than the treatment given for gapes.   On going around to shut the birds up at night is the time when the first signs can be detected, and if one will only keep their ears "open" when amongst the chicks in the evenings, how much trouble and loss might often be averted ? At first only one or two birds in a house or coop will be noticed to give a little sneeze.   The next evening when going round perhaps a dozen may be making this noise, and the next evening perhaps the whole lot are affected, and even then I have known people to let it go on and say : "Oh ! it's only a little cold ; nothing to trouble about."   Sure, 'tis nothing much at that stage, but if left, and "if the conditions are left the same," it spreads and spreads like an epidemic, and one cannot say what may be the end of it.   I have mentioned "evenings" that the sneezing is heard. This is due to the birds being together in the house, and until several get the complaint it is not so easy to detect it in the field, because when one goes around it is generally to feed, when all the birds will be hustling up for their food, and there is generally too much noise to hear one or two individuals sneeze.   And so again

Symptoms,

Sneezing.

let me say how very important it is that the poultry-keeper should keep a watch on the birds in the evenings. It is at this time when all is quiet and the chicks have gone to bed that any "foreign" noise or trouble may be heard, and the man or woman who is going to make the successful poultry breeder is the one who "scents around for danger" in the twilight of the evening—who is on the "look-out" for enemies they hope not to find. But if they are known they must be grappled with. Yes; that's the person who is going to be able to show good rearing records. There is far too much left to chance and luck in these days, and it is quite time that some of the teachers in poultry and live stock keeping took a far stronger line and told the willing pupils the great and important need of thoroughness and method, and of studying the habits of the animals under their care. If one makes a study of bird life or animal life and gets right down to Nature, what a lot may be gleaned in this way which is so very useful in the treatment and rearing of the animals.

We next find in the symptoms of catarrh in chicken a drowsy appearance, and feathers slightly ruffled. The bird will come out and eat, and in the first stages the appetite is very little affected. It will then move off to the hedge or sheltered part of the house and stand in a huddled position, eyes closed, and a dejected appearance generally. It will then suddenly wake up, and if water is near by rush off and have a heavy drink of water, and then go back and stand huddled up again. On going to the house at night when the birds are in the more advanced stage, much sneezing and coughing may be heard, as also it may be heard in the daytime when the chickens are about in the field. The house, too, will have a very unpleasant smell, and as the birds get worse the bad smell in the house increases by this time—I mean when the birds have got to this stage

Let the Poultry-keeper keep a watch in the evening.

Too much left to chance and luck.

Further Symptoms.

most poultry-keepers will have noticed that there is
something very much wrong with them, but I have
come into touch with many cases where even at this
stage nothing has been done to correct matters, the
person saying: "Oh! I knew it was a cold, but
thought it nothing much, as I have not 'lost' any birds
yet and thought they'd get over it in a week or two."
Yes, that may be; some of the birds may lose it in a
week or two, but if one was to note the loss of growth
in a mob of birds when they get this dread disease,
apart from its spreading and its several other bad
effects, they would do all in their power to stop it on
first appearance.

Treatment.

I have now given the principal symptoms, and if
one takes note, they cannot very well confound it with
any other complaint. Now comes treatment. But
may I first say, before attempting treatment, try and

Remove the
Cause.

find the cause of the outbreak, and then "Remove
the Cause." You will say, "How am I to find the
Cause?" Well, it is a very easy matter, unless it
happens to be contagion set up from some other farm
from imported birds, or by handling birds at some other
place where they were infected. This is not often the
case, and the most general cause can be found in the
rearing field and without seeking far. I will put it
in this way. We will assume we have 150 chicken
in a field, these chicken being from 8 to 12 weeks old;
they are in three houses, placed a good distance apart.
On going to shut them up for the night, we notice one
house nearly full of chicken, and one is nearly empty.
But in the rush of work, or having someone waiting to
see us, or "want of thought," we shut the birds up and
go away. The next morning, if we take the trouble
to look closely at the birds, we shall see they do not look
so bright; we shall see that some of the look as if they
have been in wet grass, especially under and about the

wings. Now, as birds do not perspire, what can this be? It is caused by the "steam" or damp heat thrown off by the bodies of the chicks, and this is what the birds have been breathing, and have had to endure for a whole night. Is it any great marvel that their lungs and their mucus membranes are affected? What would happen to a crowd of people under such conditions? Now this may not only happen *one* night, but may be going on for a week or longer, and if the weather should be showery, well, so much the worse for the poor chicks. Heat at night and wet on coming out in the morning will spell "Catarrh" in capital letters. Here, my dear readers, is the chief cause of that troublesome complaint of which I have had so much to do with during my many years work amongst poultry, and if only every ex-soldier and every new poultry woman—yes, *and* the "Old Hands"—will read and take note of this chapter, it may save them many pounds and sleepless nights—for it is a worry to a man or a woman who is rearing a number of chicken when they find the whole mob going wrong, and perhaps do not know how to combat the disease or trouble.

Now to go on with the treatment. Remove the cause by dividing the birds; by giving more sleeping accommodation; by using a better class house, with ample ventilation. Disinfect all premises, inside of Disinfect. houses; spray the ground around the house; move the birds at once to fresh quarters, if this is at all possible. I know many times this is not possible, but it saves much trouble in getting quit of the disease if such can be done. Carbolic acid, made up as given in a previous chapter and sprays with a syringe, is a very useful form of disinfectant. Keep all feeding troughs clean and water vessels clean, with fresh water always before them if water is given, as the disease gives much fever, and the birds will be drinking a lot of water if they can get it. A little permanganate of potash in the water is cleansing, but does not, as so many people think, Feed well. "cure" the birds. Feed the birds on good sound food, and give them as much as they will clear up; but if the disease gets advanced they will eat very little, and so soon get weak. But, as I have previously pointed out, in the early stages the appetite is good, so again it is another reason why the birds should be treated immediately the trouble is seen.

"A Sussex Remedy." As I have before stated, it is a complaint not easy to stamp out when it has been allowed to get a hold upon the birds, but the following is one of the best remedies that I have ever used, and I may say that I have tested a great number of so called "cures," etc., with negative results. This remedy is simple, and if carried out with care one need have no losses and the birds will soon be clear from the "pus" and inflammation. The operation must be carried out when the birds are in the house, in the morning before letting them out is a good time; get some flowers of sulphur and an old shovel, set the sulphur alight after putting a spoonful upon the shovel and place it in the house amongst the chicken so that the fumes can go all around them, if the house is very airy some sacks should be thrown over so that the fumes may be kept inside, the action of the fumes will make the birds cough and sneeze and they must be watched to see if the weaker ones fall and get trodden down; these can be taken out and given fresh air; with care in using not a chick need be lost, and have I seen some very bad cases cured with three applications of sulphur used in this way.

I have given considerable space to this troublesome complaint because up to the present I have never seen it dealt with in any practical way for the poultry keeper, and knowing as I do so well, the awful consequences of the complaint and its ravages in the poultry yard if neglected, and again that so many people are to-day taking up poultry keeping for the first time; that is my reason for making such lengthy reading.

CHAPTER XL.

VERTIGO.

There is a rather common trouble sometimes seen in young growing cockerels which I think I should like to mention, more especially as I have noticed it rather more particularly in our strong growing ''Sussex'' chickens—Vertigo. It may cause death, it may only be a short attack and the bird is soon all right again; however, it may be well to mention here that it is a sign of good feeding, or, perhaps, I should say, ''strong feeding,'' hence the reason we see it more often in a batch of growing table chicken.

Symptoms. The symptoms of this trouble cannot be mistaken when once seen; it appears as follows: generally first seen in chicken, age 8 to 16 weeks—sometimes adult birds get it. The bird will be seen to hold its head over on one side and in moving will spin around; it will recover for a few minutes and then have another attack. The trouble is due to high feeding, often caused by using too much animal food, and owing to high blood pressure on the brain the bird loses control of its actions. Sometimes a form of congestion will bring on vertigo, but in such a case it does not last long. Cure. It may be cured by lower feeding, a few Glauber Salts, and keep the bird in a quiet and somewhat darkened place.

THE REVISED (1920) STANDARDS FOR SUSSEX.

GENERAL CHARACTERISTICS OF COCK.

Head and Neck.	Head	.. ..	Medium Size.
	Beak ..	.. ..	Short and strong (curved).
	Eye ..	.. ..	Full and bright.
	Comb	.. ..	Single, medium size, evenly serrated and erect, and fitting close to the head.
	Face ..	.. ..	Red.
	Earlobes and Wattles		Of medium size.
	Neck..	.. ..	Gracefully curved, with fairly full hackle.
Body.	Breast	.. ..	Broad and square, carried well forward, with long and deep breast bone.
	Shoulders	.. ..	Wide.
	Back ..	.. ..	Broad and flat.
	Wings	.. ..	Carried close to the body.
	Skin ..	.. ..	Clear and fine in texture.
Tail. ..	.. .. ..	..	Moderate size, carried at an angle of 45°.
Legs and Feet.	Thighs	.. ..	Short and stout.
	Shanks	.. ..	Short and strong and rather wide apart; free from feathers.
	Toes	.. ..	Four in number, straight and well spread.
General Shape and Carriage.	..	.. ..	Graceful and erect, and showing long back.
Size and Weight.	..	.. ..	Large; 9lb. and upwards.
Plumage.	..	.. ..	Close.

GENERAL CHARACTERISTICS OF HEN.

Head, Neck and Body.	..	As in the Cock.
Tail.		Small, curved backwards, otherwise as in the Cock.
Legs and Feet. ..	..	As in the Cock.
General Shape and Carriage	.. ..	Graceful and erect and showing long back.
Size and Weight. ..	..	Large; 7 lb. and upwards.
Plumage.	..	Close.

GENERAL CHARACTERISTICS IN BOTH SEXES.

Beak	..	White or horn colour.
Comb, face, earlobes, and wattles	..	Red.
Shanks and feet	..	White.
Skin and flesh	..	White and fine.

COLOUR IN THE RED VARIETY.

Eye	Red.
Under Colour ..	Slate.

In the Cock.

(Plumage)	Head and neck hackle	Rich dark red striped with black
	Body	Rich dark red, one uniform shade throughout.
	Wings	Rich dark red, with black in flights.
	Wing bow	Rich dark red.
	Tail coverts	Glossy black.
	Tail	Black.

In the Hen.

	Head and Neck ..	Rich dark red, striped with black.
	Wings	Rich dark red, with black in flights.
	Tail	Black.
	Remainder of Plumage	Rich dark red, free from pepperiness.

COLOUR IN THE LIGHT VARIETY.

In both Sexes. Eye .. .. .. Orange.

In the Cock. ... Head and neck hackle — White striped with black, the black centre of each feather to be entirely surrounded by a white margin.

	Wings	White with black in flights.
	Tail coverts	Black.
	Tail	Black.
	Remainder of plumage	Pure white throughout.

In the Hen.

	Head and neck hackle	As in Cock.
	Wings	White with black in flights.
	Tail	Black.
	Remainder of plumage.	Pure white throughout.

COLOUR IN THE SPECKLED VARIETY.

In both Sexes. Eye .. .. .. Red.

In the Cock. Head and neck hackle — Rich dark mahogany striped with black and tipped with white.

	Wings	Wing bow speckled ; Primaries, white, brown and black.
	Saddle hackle ..	Similar to neck hackle.
	Tail	Sickle feathers, black with white tips. Main tail feathers black and white.

In the Cock.	Remainder of plumage	Rich dark mahogany, each feather tipped with a small white spot, a narrow glossy black bar dividing the white from the remainder of feather, and shewing the three colours distinctly, neither of the colours to run into each other, undercolour slate and red with a minimum of white.
In the Hen.	Head, neck and body	Ground colour rich dark mahogany, each feather tipped with a small white spot, a narrow glossy black bar dividing the white from the remainder of feather, the mahogany part of feather to be free from pepperiness, neither of the colours to run into each other and to shew the three colours distinctly under colour slate and red with a minimum of white.
	Tail	Black and brown with white tip.
	Flights	Black, brown and white.

COLOUR IN THE BROWN VARIETY.

In both Sexes.	Beak	Dark or horn colour.
	Eye	Brown or Red.
	Face and earlobes ..	Red.
	Shanks and feet ..	White.
	Skin and flesh ..	White and fine.
	Head and neck hackle	Rich dark mahogany striped with black.
In the Cock.	Saddle hackle ..	Same as neck hackle.
	Back and wing bow..	Rich dark mahogany.
	Wing coverts forming the Bar	Blue Black.
	Wing secondaries and flights	Black, edged with brown.
	Breast, tail and thighs	Black.
In the Hen.	Nead and neck hackle	Brown striped with black.
	Back and wings ..	Dark motley brown.
	Breast and underbody	Pale wheaten brown.
	Flights	Black, edged with brown.
	Tail	Black.

VALUE OF POINTS IN SUSSEX.

Defects	Deduct up to
Defects in Head and Comb	10
,, Colour	20
Want of Type and flatness of back	25
,, Condition	10
Defects in Legs and Feet	15
Want of Size	20
A perfect Bird to Count	**100**

Serious Defects, for which Birds should be passed—Other than four toes, wry tail, or any deformity, feather on shanks, rose comb.

The Changes in above Standards do not come into force until 1921.

S. C. SHARPE,
Hon. Secretary
Meadham, Lewes.

Lightning Source UK Ltd.
Milton Keynes UK
UKOW06f0939141217
314453UK00009B/886/P